A Dictionary of Nicknames

A Dictionary
of
Nicknames

BY

JULIAN FRANKLYN

BRITISH BOOK CENTRE
NEW YORK

© Copyright 1962 Julian Franklyn
First published in the United States of America 1963 by
The British Book Centre, Inc. (publishers)
122 East 55th Street, New York 22, New York

Library of Congress Catalog Card No. 63-10444

Printed and bound in Great Britain

Dedicated
to the memory of
'Charlie'
(Charles Brooks
Obit. 2 Dec. 1960)

The world gave to him nothing
but he gave generously of love.

CONTENTS

PREFACE

THE author's first step in the production of a book of this kind is to set the limits of the task. Having done that he must be prepared to forgive himself for an occasional trespass beyond those bounds.

This dictionary will not deal with the nicknames of organizations, such as Regiments; nor with those of places, such as Towns; nor with those of established amenities, such as regularly running Railway Trains.

In it will not be found the nicknames of historic characters except when these have been transferred from the original bearer to all men having similar peculiarities.

This is an attempt to record the robust, kindly, pertinent nicknames given by the man in the street to his mate: to classify them and, as far as possible, define them and indicate their origins and the social limits of their usage.

Inseparable nicknames are those that attach to a certain surname, 'Shiner' Wright, 'Tug' Wilson: *inevitable nicknames* are those that follow physical (or other) peculiarities, 'Ginger', 'Hoppy', 'Slasher'. *General nicknames* is an elastic term that must expand to contain all the others in common use that do not qualify for the previous groups.

There is, however, a limit beyond which a category cannot be stretched; hence, in addition, this dictionary contains terms of address, and terms of reference, but there are no boundaries beyond those self-imposed, and one word may do duty in two or even in three (or more) categories.

'Professor' is a term of address that a Cockney may use to any person whom he judges to be likely to respond to it: it may be a term of reference used between Cockneys (possibly preceded by 'the old'); or it may be a direct nickname.

In each category there are variants: how many different nicknames are there for a fool? how many for a man named Smith? The reverse reference at the end of this volume can reveal such surface figures, but there are no means of knowing whether one Smith is expected, on occasions, to answer to more than one inseparable nickname: even one's most prolific and informative 'informants' cannot solve this problem; nevertheless, I must record my indebtedness to them for the patience they have displayed in answering so many of my (what must have seemed silly) questions.

In a different category of thanks and at the top of the list stands Eric Partridge, who not only suggested my writing this book, but helped continually with advice, and with references.

Wilfred Granville was my key to the Royal Navy, and, lastly, I wish to thank Iona and Peter Opie for permitting me to reprint the modern nicknames used by children, from *The Lore and Language of School-children*; Sir Anthony Richard Wagner (Her Majesty's Garter King of Arms) for permission to quote from his masterly work, *English Genealogy*; as well as The Clarendon (Oxford University) Press, the publishers of both of these books.

I look forward to an opportunity of thanking critics and correspondents for the corrections and additions to the second edition.

Finally, immediately before going to press, I am pleased to be able to record my indebtedness to Mr. Douglas Hill, who patiently read, and expertly corrected, the proofs.

London, 1962.   J.F.

INTRODUCTION

NICKNAMES are older than surnames, and they are stronger: the relationship is something like that between parent and offspring, for nicknames begat many English surnames.

Camden, in his *Remains Concerning Britain* (1605) was the first to set surnames up as a subject for scientific investigation: 'His brief essay, weak as it necessarily is from the philological point of view, gives by far the clearest and most sensible introduction to the subject that has yet been penned,' says Professor Ernest Weekley, in *Surnames* (first published 1916, third edition 1936).

After Camden, for roughly two hundred and fifty years, nothing worthy of note came from the Press, but in 1842 *English Surnames: an Essay on Family Nomenclature*, by Mark Anthony Lower, made its appearance and was (like most of Lower's other works) so well received that it grew in girth as one edition followed another until the fourth edition, published in 1875, necessitated two volumes.

Nothing succeeds like success, and nothing exceeds like excess. Both are true of Lower. Between the first and the fourth edition of *English Surnames* he produced *Patronymica Britannica* (1860), an extensive Dictionary of Surnames containing twelve thousand entries.

Having thus given credit where credit is due, one's conscience is clear in adding that Mark Anthony, notwithstanding his M.A. and his F.S.A., was not a scholar. He was a prolific writer, and one with scholarly leanings and antiquarian interests: he was an eclectic, with no conception of research. His etymologies were merely guesswork; he 'traced' to far-fetched imaginary origins, surnames that a glance at a gazetteer would have shown him were those of the villages from which ancestors had come. His deviation is like that of the traveller who, confident of his 'instinctive' sense of direction, does not, when crossing the desert, consult the compass.

Lower's preoccupation with onomastics was too superficial for him to make a mission of it: but Robert Ferguson, who followed him, was deep, depressing, philo-Teutonic and determined to convert all men to the belief that surnames are German. He, like all monomaniacs, overdid it. He ended his career in the House of Commons.

Some English surnames are indeed Teutonic in origin: others,

French; not a few are Hebrew, but the majority are simply National, and all derived from localities, from occupations, from relationships, from personal peculiarities and, quite importantly, from nicknames.

What is a nickname? Everybody knows what a nickname is, but few could define it: even the *Oxford English Dictionary* has a chink in its armour: 'Nickname [later form of eke-name]. A name or appellation added to, or substituted for, the proper name of a person, place, etc., usually given in ridicule or pleasantry.' That, as far as it goes, is beyond reproach, but it does not go far enough. Nicknames are not by-names, nor are they to-names; they are not pet names, neither are they diminutives, all or any of which may be added to, or substituted for, proper names.

C. L'Estrange Ewen, in *A History of Surnames of the British Isles* (1931), poses the rhetorical questions; 'Is a nickname an additional or an alternative title? Is it of temporary or permanent nature? Is it dispensable or indispensable?' He then proceeds through several pages answering these questions, but whether the conclusions he reaches will be acceptable to the bulk of philologists is not certain: his aim seems to be that of showing how wrong it is to trace back to nicknames a large number of surnames that are so traced by others.

His definition is not conclusive. 'According to etymologists,' he says, 'the word nickname is a corruption of "an ekename" (i.e. an added name . . .).'

One signing himself E.G.R. contributing to *Notes and Queries* 22 March 1856 says: 'Mr. Lawrence's reference to Mr. Bellenden Ker (*Arch. Popular Phrases*, vol i, p. 184) only gives the unsatisfactory explanation "*Nuck*, a sly wink, scoff," etc. Dr. Johnson refers to the French "Nom de nique". Bailey explains it "nicht name".

'Is it not a little strange that all philologists should have overlooked the derivation in The *Promptorium Parvulorum* "Neke name or eke name, Agnomen". As the learned Editor observes, "There can be little doubt that the word is formed simply by prosthesis, the final *n* being transferred from the *article* to the substantive." ' This is no doubt quite true, but it does not help a great deal.

One of the faults of the learned and the lofty-minded is the loss of contact with mortal men. None of the pundits condescends to explain that *eke* means '*also*'. (In the Shetland Islands it is pronounced 'Ockname'.)

C. W. Bardsley's *Dictionary of English and Welsh Surnames* (1901) was the first work based on documentary evidence: it is a high peak of scholarship and research which acts as a guide to later workers in the field who build on Bardsley's foundations and rectify, in the light of modern learning, his errors. As far as the etymology of names is concerned this is not an outstanding feat. Bardsley based his conclusions on the work of Skeat, which is now a veritable museum piece. Ewen, however, is iconoclastic, he disputes Bardsley's classifications: for example, he shows that the Anglo-Saxons gave the names of animals to their children, hence animal names were not originally nicknames, and that Bardsley's estimate of ten per cent is far too high. The students must be on guard against the brooms of the controversialists who sweep each other aside: some animal names may be derived from Anglo-Saxon, others from nicknames: the latter are probably in the majority since few English surnames are of Saxon origin. In his recent book, *English Genealogy* (1960), Sir Anthony Richard Wagner, Her Majesty's Garter King of Arms, says, 'It is with the Normans that family surnames come into the English picture. They must be distinguished from personal surnames such as are found among the Vikings, whether patronymics (Godred Olafsson, Egil Skallagrimsson) or descriptive nicknames (Harold Fairhair, Thorstein the Red, Ivar the Boneless, Eric Bloodaxe) which did not pass from father to son. Such names become family names only when the son of a Richard Basset (short [of stature]) or Grimbald Pauncefote (paunch face) uses his father's nickname as his own surname merely because it was his father's; or when the son of a William FitzAlan (Son of Alan) is himself known as William FitzAlan (instead of William FitzWilliam).

'By far the greatest number of Norman surnames, however, are local, deriving from the family's place of origin or its chief lordship. A certain number of Norman families (Stafford, Grisley, Clifford, and perhaps Clinton and Montagu) took their surnames from English lordships or homes acquired after the Conquest, but the majority, at least of those whose Norman origin can be proved, derive their names from places in France.'

Sir Anthony is referring to names of the feudal rulers, not those of the people: even our kings can be called by nicknames—*Longshanks*, *Lackland*: and far famed *Plantagenet* is but a pun.

Surnames in our sense—hereditary family names—are not evident in London before about A.D. 1400, and though their frequency increased, the custom had not become universal in the Metropolis even by 1500. Two centuries later, in rural places, surnames were often not in use.

Men, and their wives, and their children, were likely to be known by a nickname having reference to personal appearance, physical characteristics, occupation, season of nativity, or incidents with which they or their ancestors were connected. The principle is exemplified in the Sagittarius being attributed as Armorial Bearings to King Stephen because he was born under that sign of the Zodiac.

Ernest Weekley in *Surnames* has four chapters on Nicknames as origins, two on Place names, and one only on each of the other formatives. In *The Romance of Names* he says: 'Every family name is etymologically a nickname, i.e. an eke-name, intended to give that auxiliary information which helps in identification.'

Dr. P. H. Reaney, whose *A Dictionary of British Surnames* (1958), as well as being the most up-to-date, is the most authoritative, says (in his learned and enlightening 'Introduction'): 'that many modern surnames were originally nicknames is proved conclusively by the material in the following pages,' but he is careful not to overstate his case. He makes it clear that the very nature of a nickname may make it unintelligible, and the reason for its bestowal may not be traceable since it was not a conscious effort.

The present writer was, during the Second War, known to all ranks as 'Felix', but no amount of careful (guarded) inquiry could reveal when, why, how, or by whom the nickname was bestowed. This failure to gain enlightenment arose not from any delicacy of feeling in those who might have been in possession of the facts; for, as Michael Harrison pointed out in *Reported Safe Arrival* (irrespective of which branch of the Service one is in), 'even your best friends *will* tell you'. The reason why the nickname 'Felix' remained unaccounted for was simply because the man who originated it did not himself realize he had done so.

Dr. Reaney's attitude to the problem is a refreshing one: it has elasticity and flexibility: it neither defines nor circumscribes, it draws the line freehand rather than with the ruler.

The system of hereditary family surnames is now common to all classes of the population, and is too firmly established for the social factors that were formative—if they still exist—to have any further effect, but the bestowal of nicknames is so spontaneous, so fundamental a factor of social intercourse, that it can and does in these days and within a restricted area, and for the duration of a period of time, take precedence over surname, personal name, and even over title or rank.

Nicknames can kill or caress—a cutting nickname that 'catches on' can put a man out of politics more permanently than can a misdemeanour on his part: the nickname of a national hero may maintain him in office long after his abilities have waned. The form they take may vary from a polite, almost a classic, phrase to one vulgar, even obscene, word. Nicknames may be private or they may be public: in fact, the field is so wide that it seems endless, and he who wanders in it must, sooner or later, be guilty of trespass; for no boundaries are marked, no fences have been erected: when is a nickname not a nickname? When, for example, does a slang term of description stop being a descriptive term and become a nickname? No philologist has, so far, attempted to sift the material.

Albert R. Frey published in 1887 a work entitled *Sobriquets and Nicknames*. He made no pretence of doing more than collect: his work is without an introduction, and the Preface is less than one page in length. He says: 'We are informed that in the fourteenth century the word *sobriquet* was employed to express a sound of contempt, "half whistle and half jeer". . . . In the course of time the term has undergone some modifications, and the reader of today [1887], no matter to what especial branch of literature or history he may devote himself, must have encountered these peculiar nicknames. . . . It appears somewhat strange that no book has yet been issued which is devoted to the explanation and derivation of these witty, and, in some instances, abusive, appellations. . . .'

He then proceeds with his dictionary which is a most valuable source of information on such nicknames as:

ACCOMPLISHED, THE: A sobriquet conferred on John Gaetano Orisini, Pope Nicholas III. . . .

ACHILLES OF ENGLAND, THE: A name bestowed on Arthur Wellesley, Duke of Wellington.

CITIZEN KING, THE: A name given to Louis Philippe of France, because the citizens of Paris elected him in 1830.

KING OF PHRASES, THE: A name given to George Louis Le Clerc, Comte de Buffon, the French naturalist. . . .

TRAGAEDIOGRAPHUS. So Francis Meres, in his *Palladis Tamia* calls Michael Drayton.

Thus we see that Frey's work was learned, literary and polite, as indeed it had to be in 1887.

Nothing that was not a watering down of Frey made its appearance until 1904 when *A Dictionary of Names, Nicknames and Surnames*, by Edward Latham, appeared. This, again, is a useful book, but is rather a mixture. The author says: 'Although the title may afford a better notion of the nature of its contents than seems to be the case in most of the existing works containing similar information, yet it may not be out of place to mention their general scope. In these pages will be found a selection of names, nicknames and surnames of noted persons, places and things (unless, as often happens, they are self-explanatory), comprising cities, districts, counties, popular resorts, old coffee-houses, taverns, gardens, theatres, monuments, prisons, bridges, tunnels, ships, rivers, walls, acts of parliament, laws, parliaments, diets, councils, alliances, treaties, battles, wars, peaces, armies, guns, anniversaries, eras, periods, ages, governments, political parties, ceremonies, moons, dogs, saints, exploits, offices (dignities), companies, schemes, trials, conspiracies, insurrections, instruments of torture, railway engines, newspapers, periodicals, prizes, lectures, races, societies, clubs, sects, Orders of Knighthood, famous diamonds, nuggets, animals and trees.'

Can he be serious? Does he mean all that? Well—yes: but with such a list, there is room, in one small volume, for but a few in each category.

The noteworthy dictionaries of general slang that have from time to time made their appearance have automatically included a few nicknames, but it was not until Eric Partridge's *Dictionary of Slang and Unconventional English* made its appearance in 1937 that any serious attempt was manifested to emphasize and, to some extent, classify, the rollicking nicknames that glitter like gems in the everyday speech of the ordinary people.

So determined do philologists seem to ignore the fact that language is made in the market, not in the cloisters, that one experiences something of a shock to read in Ewen's work: 'Some epithets are bestowed upon every person of the same name; for instance, any John Clark who enlists in the Army is forthwith known as "Nobby" Clark, and every James or other Miller who goes to sea is henceforth called "Dusty" Miller. "Nobby" and "Dusty" are true nicknames used as alternatives to John and James, but they are generic, common to numerous Clarks and Millers respectively.'

That is a great unbending. Ewen does not mean that Nobby can be applied only to a Clark whose personal name is John. That, of course, is quite wrong. Such nicknames as Nobby and Dusty are in no way related to the personal names, but have become inseparably attached to the appropriate surnames.

Ewen is, alas, misleading in implying that Nobby belongs to the Army, and Dusty to the Navy; the majority (if not the total) of these inseparable nicknames are used lavishly in both the Army and the Navy and, as the various mechanized units have grown upon us, in the other Services. It is probable but, so far, unprovable, that the system started in the Navy, and it does not seem to be older than mid-nineteenth century.

Inevitable nicknames, those bestowed upon a man because of his personal appearance, or physical characteristics, such as, for example, 'Ginger', or 'Hoppy', are far older, and are not of Service origin. General nicknames, particularly those that refer to a man's place of birth, as, for example, 'Yorkie', 'Cockney', 'Jock', 'Paddy', are older still: are, in fact, the most prevalent type of nickname that gave rise to so many English surnames.

Dialect words, and slang words that are primarily descriptive, may also be employed as nicknames for the people they are used to describe: the village idiot is *a softie*, he most likely answers to the name of 'Softie'.

Many nicknames that sound to the polite ear offensive, even cruel, are not so intended, and the person who answers to them does not feel himself either insulted or hurt. Nicknames bestowed with the intention to wound are more common to the educated than to the uneducated, although the latter keep a reserve of insulting national and local nicknames for use when quarrels are in progress.

The usage of nicknames is predominantly masculine. Although men have their nicknames for women, they seldom call the women by them, and, except in the underworld, it is uncommon for women to address each other by any nickname except those bordering on diminutives or on pet names.

Personal and private nicknames usually emerge in the family circle during infancy, and, as a rule, are used (perhaps for life) only by relations and intimate friends. Sometimes such a nickname escapes the narrow circle and becomes known and used by acquaintances, even by strangers: such a process has been formative of some of the inseparable nicknames in use today—see, for example, 'Tug Wilson', in the following onomasticon.

The process has been known to go even further and a nickname has become standard (or near standard) English. *Grog* is a word that is perhaps not employed in the best circles, but is one that will shock no one. Of it, Eric Partridge says: 'Rum diluted: 1770. — 2. Spirits and water: from *c.* 1790.—3 Strong drink in gen[eral] from *c.* 1820. Orig[inally] s[lang], all these senses were coll[oquial] by 1840, S[tandard] E[nglish] by 1870? Ex *grogram*, whence *Old Grog*, the nickname of Admiral Vernon who, in the summer of 1740, ordered the Navy's rum to be diluted and who wore a grogram cloak. . . .'

Among Public Nicknames are those of regiments, of ships, of towns —particularly the last. Is there anyone in the United Kingdom who does not know that *Pompey* is Portsmouth, but is there anyone who can say why? Who would not recognize *Brum* as Birmingham? The origin of *Brum* is not far to seek, but to the average man there is no difference in character between the two terms, yet no man from Portsmouth is ever nicknamed 'Pompey' but many men from Birmingham answer to 'Brum'.

The transference of the nickname of a place to the inhabitants is operative in the United States of America as well as in Britain, and it is no new fashion. One signing himself *Vespertilio*, writing in *Notes and Queries*, 18 October 1856, says: 'In *English Traits* Emerson says (p. 27): "I chanced to read Tacitus *On the Manners of the Germans*, not long since in Missouri and the heart of Illinois, and I found abundant points of resemblance between the Germans of the Hercynian forest and our *Hoosiers*, *Suckers*, and *Badgers*, of the American woods."

'I am told that the three words printed in italics are the nicknames given by the Americans to the inhabitants of three of the States of the Union (for instance, that by "Suckers" the inhabitants of Illinois are meant). Can any of your readers furnish me with a complete list of similar nicknames in use in the United States to designate the inhabitants of each State?'

It seems that none of the readers of *Notes and Queries* could answer the question then, and it is open to doubt whether anyone could be complete and authoritative on the matter now. Even H. L. Mencken, in his masterly work *The American Language*, does not give the required information. He lists the nicknames of the States, but he does not indicate whether the people carry the same nickname, or whether they carry some other nickname common to all inhabitants of the particular State. It is further difficult (if not impossible) to discover how far the nicknames applied to natives and inhabitants of certain States are in current use, and how far they have a literary existence only, and of those that really are alive, how many are 'national'? and if local only, in which American locality are they used?

One treads upon dangerous ground in defining the usage of nicknames at home, without venturing abroad. Customary usage in one part of the country may be contrary to the common usage in another. The witty, verbal, mercurial-minded Cockney is far more apt at the forging of new, and redistribution of old, nicknames than is the inhabitant of some rural parts of the country; it is possible, therefore, that one who is conversant with Cockney peculiarities of speech will make the error of assuming that a term of reference, being a dialect word, may be employed as a nickname in its own county. This is a risk one has to run, because it is impossible to check one's conclusions:

the elusive nickname slips through the fingers of the scholars; those novelists who are a wealth of information on slang are not so prolific on nicknames simply because even if every character in a book has one, there are but few characters.

'Social Workers' are, in the main, a menace. Miss Ecks, who wrote *My Six Sad Months in Soul-Starved Stepney*, says that the mild little man who would not have hurt a fly was called 'Slasher' but she could not find out why. What she did not discover either is that the Cockney is a gentleman. Both of these revelations await the lady: she has but to look up 'Slasher' in the following Glossary.

The making and the giving of nicknames is as primordial as is the making and giving of any names: it is a fundamental factor in the growth of language. This is indicated by the most prolific production and persistent use being found among children. No parent, no teacher —nor any other adult—has ever set up a class to teach tiny tots to be rude to each other, but they are most apt: their facility in that direction is exceeded by their withering ability to brand teachers and others with a nickname that irritates, that he or she is permitted to know, but about which nothing can be done. Iona and Peter Opie, in their recent book *The Lore and Language of Schoolchildren*, have indicated, even if they have not said this: they have also made it clear that children have more uncomplimentary nicknames for the policeman than criminals have.

Another service their work has rendered to linguistics is that of establishing a date of emergence for all the modern words, and indicating an approximate date for some of the older terms. Dating is demanded in modern lexicography, but with nicknames for material it seems wiser to fail the avid date-seeker than to mislead him. With many nicknames there is no extraneous evidence to indicate a probable date; with others, particularly those that began life as descriptive terms and subsequently assumed the status of nicknames, a date will refer to the first discovered recording of the word, not to the first time it was printed in its new activity: it is a problem of semantics that cannot be solved, and should not be made subject to supposition.

Chronological inadequacy is magnified by the number of nicknames glossed herein that have been gathered by 'field work', in the cafés surrounding the great London markets, in unglamorous corners of Soho, in the strange places where buskers and pavement-artists congregate. These raucous, robust boys know numerous names, but not necessarily even today's date.

In the underworld there are no names, only nicknames: in the half-world of the neither criminal nor respectable, nicknames are used, but surnames may be known: in the markets, and among costers and other street-traders, perfectly polite and normal names are known, prefaced with a 'Mr.', and so used in public, but to address one in private by anything but a nickname is considered 'uppish' and unfriendly, and so the system of familiar address thins out through the social network: nevertheless, a brilliant publicity man, without fear of giving offence, produced for the North Thames Gas Board the following fascinating advertisement:

> 'Gas Hot Water round the clock—Cock!
> Gas Hot Water does the lot.
> Sheets and Blankets, all your wash—Tosh!
> By Gas the Water's always hot.'

GLOSSARY

The following abbreviations have been used:

C. or Cent. = Century.
c.   = *circa* (about).
cf.   = *confer* (compare).
Mathews   = *A Dictionary of Americanisms* (1951) by M. M. Mathews.
q.v.   = *quod vide* (which see).
Wentworth   = *American Dialect Dictionary* (1944) by Dr. H. Wentworth.
Wentworth
& Flexner   = *Dictionary of American Slang* (1960) by Dr. H. Wentworth and S. B. Flexner.
Wright   = *The English Dialect Dictionary* (1898) by Joseph Wright.

A

Abbess: is an XVIII–XIX C. nickname for a procuress, or a brothel keeper. (The girls under her jurisdiction were sometimes nicknamed 'nuns'). In *The Lame Lover* (1770) Foote gives, 'who should trip by but an Abbess . . . with a smart little nun . . .', and in 1782 Peter Pindar (Wolcot), *Odes to the Pope*, says:

So an old Abbess, for the
    rattling rakes,
A tempting dish of human
    nature makes,
And dresses up a luscious maid.

Abdul: is a general nickname for a Turk, or anyone else of East Mediterranean origin. Chiefly Cockney usage.

Abel: is the inseparable nickname of any man named *Cain* or *Cane.*

Abie: is a nickname likely to be used in addressing any Jew, notwithstanding that the speaker knows the given, and the family name of the person so addressed. It is a reduced form of Abraham, and very common Jewish given name. Ikey (from Isaac) and Izzy (from Isadore) are both used in the same way, but less frequently. It is also a general nickname for a journeyman tailor, be he Jewish, Roman Catholic, or Greek Orthodox. Ikey has a specialized application to a mean person.

Abok see *Yabock.*

Acadian: is an American nickname for a native of Louisiana, of French ancestry. Sometimes spelt *Cagian*, and also *Cajun*.

Ados: is an Army nickname for the *Assistant Director* of Ordinance Services.

Aggie: is the inseparable nickname of any man named Weston. Of naval origin, from the name of Miss (Dame) Agnes Weston, who spent a pious lifetime and a considerable fortune in 'bettering' the lives of seamen. She opened Sailors' Homes and Temperance Bars: and wrote a book called *My Life Among the Bluejackets*. It is assumed by commissioned ranks that ratings have a reverential respect for the lady's memory, and they are deaf to the lower deck pronunciation of *Aggie Wetson*. It is also an American nickname for a student at a School of Agriculture.

Ago (pronounced ag-o): was the nickname used in the National Fire Service for an *Assistant Group Officer*. Those girls who particularly liked her, or those who wanted something, would extend it to *Agsey*.

Agsey see *Ago*.

Algy: is a general nickname for any man who takes pains to be well dressed and well groomed. From the given name *Algernon* which is considered aristocratic.

Alphabetical: the inevitable nickname of any man possessing a number of initials. Originally naval, but later spread to other Services.

Ambi: nickname used on the training ship *Conway*, for one whose conduct is too good to be true, and who is therefore suspected of being *ambitious* of gaining favours, or promotion, or both.

Amoth: Southern Irish nickname for a 'softie', a person easily dissolved to tears, a 'gossoon'.

Amy Florence: a nickname, now obsolete, formerly used in Northamptonshire for an untidy, tawdrily dressed woman.

Anie: is an endearing nickname for 'a small one'. Often a mother's nickname for the youngest child (Wright) Scotland. It 'translates' *own*, my own, my dearest.

Ankle-biter see *Midge*.

Annie Laurie: was the nickname used during the Second War for female lorry drivers.

Annie Oakley: nickname for a marksman. [On information only, hence to be accepted with reserve. Not confirmed by Mathews who gives 'A.O. (1860–1926) a noted woman marksman who travelled for seventeen years with Buffalo Bill's Wild West Show. . . .' An A.O. is American slang for a free pass into a show from its customarily having a hole in the centre.]

Ant see *Enos*.

Anzac: a term used by civilians to describe any Australian or New Zealand soldier, but not used as a form of address. A voluntary canteen worker might have said, 'We had five Anzacs in our hut last week: such handsome boys.' She would not have said, 'Here you are, Anzac—here's your tea.' The term, which was semi-official, was not employed in familiar address by the troops. It is condensed from A.N.Z.A.C., that is, *A*ustralian, and *N*ew *Z*ealand *A*rmy *C*orps. Sir Ian Hamilton, General Birdwood, and Lieut. A. T. White, Anzac H'dq'rs Clerk, are all credited with the origination of the word.

Ape: is a particularly offensive nickname used (seldom?) in U.S.A. for a Negro.

'Appy: is the inseparable nickname of all men named Day. It originates, and is now most frequently applied in, the Navy, where the inveterate grouser—irrespective of his surname, is known as ''Appy day'—generally reduced to ''Appy'.

Aptycock: is a nickname used in Devon and Cornwall for a person who is clever or nimble. From *apt*, intelligent, able, quick-witted, plus *cock* [q.v.].

Arab: is a general nickname given in U.S.A. to Jews, and Eastern Europeans, particularly when engaged in peddling, or door-to-door selling.

Arch Tiffy: one of the nicknames for the Warrant Engineer Officer in the Navy: from *ar*tifi-(cer).

Arkansawyer: is the local term for a native of Arkansas. Persons from other States say *Arkansan*.

Arpint (half pint): is a Cockney nickname for a small man.

Arso: nickname for the *A*rmament *S*upplies *O*fficer, employed chiefly by officers in the Royal Navy.

Aspro: was the nickname used in military circles, during the Second War, for the *S*ervices' *P*ublic *R*elations *O*fficer.

At: is a nickname used in military circles for a member of the *A*uxiliary *T*erritorial Service: the ATS, in which body of women a 'blondie' is styled 'the adjutant's At'.

Auguste: is the nickname for the junior clown at a circus—the 'stooge' for *Joey* [q.v.].

Auntie: is a respectful and at the same time friendly term of address to an elderly woman, not necessarily one's relation. Also employed in U.S.A.

Aussie: used by the troops, particularly during the 1914–18 war, as a friendly term of address to any Australian or New Zealand soldier, whether one was acquainted with him or not. It was never attached to a surname. It was frequently used in an adjectival setting: 'Aussie rations: Aussie pay: Aussie boots.' (Australians use it to describe their country).

B

Baas: customary term of address to the skipper of a Dutch ship.

Baby doll (generally shortened to Baby): is primarily an endearment, of American origin, used by young men to their sweethearts, and in that sense it is not eligible for inclusion: however, many 'good-time girls', having no permanent young man to use the term, assume it as a nickname, and it is thus used fairly widely between men and girls, strangers to each other, but habitués of dance-halls, and similar centres of social contact. The term, in this usage, was Anglicized soon after, or during the 1914–18 war, and the process was helped greatly by a popular song, 'You called me Baby-Doll a year ago'. Further, *Baby*, *Babs* or *Beebee* is commonly employed in families, at all social levels, both here and in U.S.A., as a nickname for the youngest—particularly if a girl—with whom it may stick for life.

Back end of a bus see *Jumbo*.

Badgers: nickname of the inhabitants of Wisconsin, U.S.A.

Bag-o'-bones see *Skinnigut*.

Bagal see *Bauchle*.

Baggies: the Army's nickname for a sailor: from the 'bell-bottom' trousers.

Bags: is a now obsolete nickname for a commercial traveller. He carried his samples in bags before the popularization of motor transport.

Baldy: is a nickname often given to a bald-headed person. It is not popular because it lacks wit, cf. *Curly*, and, for the same reason, is more likely to be resented.

Ballocks in brackets: is a term of reference to a bow-legged man, and is sometimes used in a quite inoffensive spirit, as a term of address: e.g. 'Oi—*oi*!—bollocks in brackets! 'ave a pint on me!'

Balloon see *Jumbo*.

Balls: is the inseparable nickname of any man named either Avery or Ivory. From the fact of the best billiards balls being turned from ivory, and the cheap kind, moulded in some form of 'composition', being referred to as 'ivory'.

Baltimorons: is the general nickname used in U.S.A. for natives of or inhabitants of Baltimore.

Banana: is a nickname used in U.S.A. for a Mulatto.

Bananaman: general nickname for a man from Queensland. Exclusively Australian in usage. It sometimes takes the forms *Bananalander* and *Banana-eater*.

Bandend: a nickname used in Yorkshire for a ne'er-do-well (Wright).

Bandy: nickname in the Navy and in the Royal Marines for the Bandmaster.

Bang-bang: is the inseparable nickname of any man named Cannon. It was used in the Services during the Second War and seems to have originated at that period.

Banger: nickname for any man who is knock-kneed. It originated in the Navy, but has currency among civilians.

Banker: is a nickname used by miners for one who works 'on the bank', above ground.

Bark: is a nickname given in Northumberland, to an Irishman. It is also employed in the American underworld. Perhaps from a malformation of the name Burke.

Barker: is a nickname used in Cornish mining circles, for any man with a stiff leg, hence, one who walks with a limp. From folklore: one of that name who said he did not believe in 'knockers' (mine-gnomes), found himself one day surrounded by a gang of them, who hacked his knee with their hews. There is also a Cornish catch-phrase, 'Stiff as Barker's knee'.

Barley Butt see *Muttoned*.

Barney: is the inseparable nickname for anyone named Alban, but it is used in this sense only in Australia (or by Australians). From the name of a famous bookmaker. In U.S.A. it is a general nickname for any Australian. (For 'Barney Williams' see *Bungy*.)

Baron: a now obsolete nickname for a fat man. In late XIX and early XX C. it had a local currency in Southwark, Lambeth and Bermondsey from George Parkes, the portly lessee of *The South London Music Hall* (now a waste-paper warehouse) who was himself nicknamed 'The Baron'.

Barrage-balloon see *Jumbo*.

Barrel see *Jumbo*.

Barrel-belly see *Jumbo*.

Barrow-guts see *Jumbo*.

Basher: is the inevitable nickname—preceding the surname—of a boxer whose technique is hard punching; fighting by brute force rather than boxing by skill. It is also a general nickname for a quick-tempered man who resorts to fisticuffs on but slight provocation. From *bash*, to strike; but when, as is not uncommon, it is used as a nickname for a very lively fellow, it is from *bash*, to coit, hence, for any lusty male.

Basil: is a nickname used in Liverpool for a fat man, and in Scotland for a drunkard. Also spelt *Bazil*.

Batchy: is the inseparable nickname of any man named Payne. Its use is almost exclusive to the Navy. 'Batchy' is a variation of 'batty', or 'bats', from 'Bats in the belfry'—mentally disturbed. Possibly applied to the surname because bats enter and leave the belfry by way of the panes—panels, or 'lights'.

Batesomer: is used in U.S.A. as a general nickname for people from Ireland.

Bats: is the nickname given to the Deck Landing Officer on an aircraft-carrier, from the bats he uses to signal with.

Bauchle or **Bagal**: is an Irish nickname for a person of no account: a fool, or an awkward person.

Bauson: is a dialect nickname for a gross, fat person, particularly if also stupid, and inclined to somnolence. Also spelt *Bawsin*.

Bawcock: a Yorkshire nickname for a foolish person.

Bawsin see *Bauson*.

Bay State Boys: nickname applied to the inhabitants of Massachusetts, U.S.A.

Beagles (or **Border Beagles**): is a nickname applied to the inhabitants of both Virginia and Mississippi. The initial 'B' is intrusive: the term is derived from Border *Eagle* State.

Beaky: is one of the inevitable nicknames given to a man with a big nose. Less popular than *Conky* [q.v.].

Beanie: a general nickname for any man from Leicestershire. It is a shortening of Bean-belly, from the belief that the population of Leicestershire subsist largely on beans. The same term, now obsolescent, refers to one full of vigour, but in altered form

'full-o'-beans' it is still current— in fact, popular.

Beanpole: a nickname, less popular now than in the first decade of the century, for a tall thin man.

Beardie: is a nickname, used during the XIX Cent. in America, for a Jewish convert to Christianity. Now obsolescent, if not obsolete.

Beatlasher see *Flatty*.

Beebee see *Baby*.

Beefeater: is an American nickname for an Englishman. Probably with reference to the 'Roast beef of old England' myth.

Beefhead: a general nickname used in U.S.A. for anyone from Texas. (See also *Beethead*).

Beefy: is a general nickname for a sturdy, thick-set man.

Bees-wing: nickname for a toper: used in upper-class circles, often prefixed with 'old', and invariably a term of admiration: from the film on old Port wine. In use at least as early as 1870.

Beethead: is a nickname given in the U.S.A. to one from Texas, but is probably merely an altered form of *Beefhead* [q.v.].

Beetle see *Flatty*.

Beetle-crusher see *Flatty*.

Beetroot: is one of the numerous inevitable nicknames thrust upon a person with auburn hair. Iona and Peter Opie, in *Lore and Language of Schoolchildren* (1959) give, under the sub-title of 'Redheads' (p. 170) 'Red heads attract a barrage of nicknames:...blood-nut, carroty-pow (Forfar), copper crust, coppernob, fire-bucket, fire-head, flame, flarey, foxy, fury, ginge, ginger [q.v.], ginger-conk, ginger-mop, ginger-nob, ginger-nut, Ginger Tom, gingy, glow-worm, mad-head, reddy, red-kipper, red-mop, red-thatch, red-paint-brush, Rufus, Rusty (ac-companied by hints that he was left out in the rain when a baby). He is uncoverably open to insult:' There then follows four rhymes of an uncomplimentary sort.

' "Ginger you're barmy getcher 'air cut" has been a greeting to coppernobs ever since it was a catch phrase in the Harry Cham-pion song, written by Fred Murray. . . . For all this, it is generally conceded that "Ginger for pluck" is a true saying.'

Bejan: nickname for a first-year student at a Scottish univer-sity. From the French *bejaune*, a beginner in a trade, itself from *bec jaune*, a yellow-beak, i.e. a young bird.

Belcher, Mr.: a nickname for a person who unashamedly belches.

Belgeek: is an American nick-name for a Belgian.

Bella: Cockney nickname for a woman with a loud voice which she uses incessantly. (Not for a market-woman.) From a play on English *bellow*, the loud cry of a bull, and *Bella*, Italian feminine given name, 'beautiful'.

Ben Block: is a long-obsolete nickname for any sailor: from the block, or pulley, through which tackle-rope is run.

Bessy: is a dialect nickname for a man who takes an interest in women's affairs, also for a man who does a 'comic-turn' dressed as a woman: i.e. the Dame in a pantomime.

Bessy Bunter see *Jumbo*.

Bessybabs: is a Yorkshire dialect nickname for a petu-lant, whimpering, spoilt child (Wright).

Betsy: is the inseparable nick-name of a man named Gay. It seems to be exclusive to the Royal Navy. It is said to be de-rived from a now long-forgotten music-hall song: 'That Charming Betsy Gay'.

Betty: nickname for a man who is, at home, subordinated into doing the house-work on Saturday afternoon.

Bexandebs: a general nick-name applied to young Jewish girls, particularly those free in their manner. The term, which was popular towards the end of XIX C. is now obsolescent, but not extinct: from *Beck*—short for Rebecca, and *Deb*—short for Deborah. (In modern times these fine Biblical names are being abandoned. Jewish girls are as likely to be Pams and Corals as are their Christian sisters.)

Biddy: a general nickname for an Irish girl. Francis Grose records this meaning in 1795: by 1905 it was extended to include a woman of any age, and not necessarily Irish: it has now returned to its original meaning. *Chick-a-biddy* is, however, a general term of endearment.

Biff: substitutional for Smith. It might be classified as Rhyming Slang, since it has its origin in a rhyme on *Smiff* which is the Cockney pronunciation of the name. 'Biff' is a slang-word from late XIX C. for punch, to strike, hence extended to include any activity ('I'll have a biff at it',) and also coitus.

Big-belly: is an American nickname for a Sioux Indian.

Big-belly-bump see *Jumbo*.

Big Devil: an American nickname, now obsolete, for the Assiniboine Indians.

Biged (Big head): a nickname thrust upon those whom the cap fits.

Big-knife: a nickname formerly given by the Indians to an American, particularly one from Virginia, as contrasted with an Englishman. Also *Great-knife*: *Long-knife* (Mathews). Probably so named from their carrying swords.

Big White Chief see *Paleface*.

Biggy: is a distinguishing nickname for the elder of two brothers attending Christ's Hospital contemporaneously.

Bill: is the inseparable nickname of any man named Sykes or

Sikes, throughout the Services but not common in civil life. From Dickens' famous underworld character in *Oliver Twist*.

Bill Jim: any Australian, used only by Australians. Also spelt 'Billjim'. The term was 'picked up' during the Second War by American troops. It did not 'infect' general American slang.

Billy: is one of the inseparable nicknames of men named Wells: from the prize fighter, Bombardier Billy Wells, famous in the early years of this century.

Billy-born-drunk: a nickname for an inveterate drunkard, and particularly for a drinker of methylated spirit.

Billy Bunter the Second see *Jumbo*.

Bimbo: is a general nickname used in America for a person of no importance.

Bimshar: is an American nickname for an Englishman. (Probably from *Bim-shire*; never—it seems—very popular, now obsolete.)

Binder: is the nickname given in the R.A.F. to the perpetual grouser.

Bing: is the inseparable nickname of any man named Crosby: from the American vocalist who popularized the tuneless, out-of-step type of very prosy song that has now killed real vocal merit. It must be recorded in his favour, however, that his rendering of 'Buddy, can you spare a dime?'

was most touching, particularly at that period of Western economic history when millions were unemployed, and near starvation, on both sides of the Atlantic.

Birdy: is a general nickname for any man whose surname is that of a bird, as Finch, Dove, Partridge, Sparrow; also for any man with a prominent nose.

Blackoke: is a recent (and still confined to underworld usage) term of reference to a coloured prostitute. It appears to be a play on 'oke', the condensed form of 'O.K.' and 'Oak'. There is an American underworld (low slang?) term *Black Oak*, meaning coitus between a 'white' man and a 'black' woman.

Blacky: is the inseparable nickname of any man named either Bird or Ramsay(ey).

Blad: a contemptuous nickname given in both Ireland and Scotland to a weak person.

Blanco: is the inseparable nickname of any man named White. From *Blanco*, a labour-saving cleaning material, first marketed to the Army in 1895. It is not derived from the name of Blanco White, poet and theologian (d. 1841), 'the troops'—and the average civilian—never having heard of him.

Blatherskite: is the American form of *Bletherskate* [q.v.] and is also current in Australia.

Blemish: is an American nickname for a Belgian. According to

A. A. Roback, *A Dictionary of International Slurs* (1946), a portmanteau word: 'Belgian' and 'Flemish'.

Bletherskate: is a term of reference to, and a general nickname for, an indiscreet, talkative or garrulous person. Of Scottish origin, it can be traced back to XVII C.

Blimp: is a nickname given to a fat little girl. The term, which does not seem to be used extensively, has its origin in the bulky and quite graceless barrage-balloons used in defence against air-attack during the Second War.

Blossom: is a humorous Cockney nickname for a singularly unattractive girl or woman.

Blowze: a nickname applied to a fat, coarse, untidy woman. Shakespeare has 'Sweet blouse, you are a beauteous blossom, sure.' *Titus A.* IV, ii, 72. *Bousy*, which is perhaps merely a different shape of the same word, and having the same meaning, is used in various parts of England.

Blucher: is the nickname given to a junior prefect—one in half power: a blucher is a half boot, as worn by the Prussian Field-Marshal. The term is used only in Winchester School, and is now obsolescent.

Blue (or **Blue-gum**): an obsolete American nickname for a negro. It is still employed as a descriptive term for a particularly dark-skinned negro.

Bluebottle: a nickname for a Bluecoat boy, used by the Bluecoat girls at Hertford School. It is also a general nickname for a policeman.

Blueboy see *Flatty*.

Blue hen (or **Blue hen's chick**): is a nickname given in U.S.A. to a native of, or an inhabitant of, Delaware.

Bluejacket see *Flatty*.

Blue-lamp-boy see *Flatty*.

Blue Nose: is the general nickname of anyone from either Nova Scotia or New Brunswick, but particularly for a sailor. It is also employed in U.S.A. as a nickname for a puritanical person.

Blues: one of the nicknames applied to the inhabitants of New Jersey, U.S.A.

Blueskin: a nickname applied to a Presbyterian. Current in the U.S.A. down to the end of the XIX Cent., in which sense it is now obsolescent. The term was derived from *Blue Laws*, the rigid and intolerant code of New England. It is a current nickname for a negro.

Blind Tom: is a nickname for the umpire of a baseball game. In American racing circles it is applied to a track-steward.

Blinker: is the inseparable nickname of any man named Hall. Current chiefly in the Navy: from 'Blinker Hall of N.I.D. in the First War who forestalled most of Germany's naval moves and ran Roger Casement to earth' ex a letter (2 March 1960) to the author from Wilfred Granville.

Blinkers: is a nickname given in the Navy to anyone who wears spectacles, which aids to vision are not below the standard of physical fitness demanded for certain ranks—for example, Paymasters.

Blinky: is a nickname given in the American underworld to a blind man, or to one who feigns blindness when begging.

Bloater (or **Yarmouthbloater**): is a term of reference to, and a nickname for, any native or inhabitant of Yarmouth.

Bloke, The: nickname for a senior (commanding) officer in both the Royal and the Merchant Navies: in the former the Commander: in the latter, the (First) Mate.

Blondy: applied to any man, irrespective of surname, with fair hair: Blondy Smith, Blondy Jones, Blondy Robinson: and in personal address: ''ere, Blondy, got a fag?' Naval in origin, and carried to a limited extent into civil life.

Bloodnut see *Beetroot*.

Blood-tub see *Jumbo*.

Blunther: is a nickname for 'a person of hasty temper and unguarded speech' (Wright). Probably from *blunt*. To refer to a person of either sex as *John Blunt* expresses the same idea although a hasty temper is generally not involved—frank, outspoken.

Blunty: is a nickname given to a person of inferior mental power, a stupid person. Scottish dialect.

Boats: Naval nickname for the ship's boats-officer.

Bob: is a nickname for anyone with whom the speaker is friendly. Usage is confined to Essex, and people from Essex. With a final 's', *Bobs*, it was the nickname of Lord Roberts. There are two influences at work in its formation. 'Bobs Bahadur' is Hindustani for *hero*, or *Champion*, and it was a title of respect and admiration employed by Indian troops. Bob is the diminutive of the given name Robert hence *Bobs*, *Roberts*, and was an expression of affection used by English troops.

Bobby: nickname for a Police Constable: from the given name of Sir Robert Peel, who introduced both *The Peace Preservation Act 1814* and *The Metropolitan Police Act 1828*, but before 1828, according to Farmer and Henley (*Slang and its Analogues*—7 vols. 1890–1904) 'a guardian of a public square or other open space' was called a Bobby, short for Bobby the Beadle—also the Proctors at both Oxford and Cambridge.

Bobby Atkins: is a rare alternative (or a mistaken) form of *Tommy Atkins* [q.v.].

Bod: is a now obsolete Scottish nickname for a short man.

Bodger: is the inseparable nickname of all men named Lees. Possibly from 'botcher'.

Bogey: is the inseparable nickname of anyone named Harris. 'Bogey' is early XIX C. slang for (*a*) a landlord; (*b*) a policeman; (*c*) the Devil, hence there may have been a notorious seamen's lodging-house named Harris'. (See also *Chats*.) Second in frequency of occurrence, Bogey is, if not quite an inseparable, a very frequent nickname for any man named Knight. From that demon of the night, the bogey-man, invoked by misguided mothers and nurses who thus induced in their victims violent attacks of *pavor nocturnus*, in the mistaken belief that fear-rigor was a symptom of sound sleep.

Boghedy: is an Irish dialect nickname for a cripple.

Bohunk: is a nickname used in U.S.A. and Canada for a Polish or Hungarian workman. Probably from a blend of *Bohe*mian and *Hun*garian.

Boily: is a Yorkshire dialect nickname for a farm labourer.

Bojer: a British Army nickname for a Boer: used during the South African War, now obsolete.

Bokanky: is a nickname used only in Durham, and chiefly by schoolboys, for a coward. From the name of Dr. Walter Balcanqual, Dean of Durham, who fled from the city during the Civil War.

Boker: is a shape of next entry:

Boko: one of the nicknames likely to be bestowed upon any man with a prominent nose. The term is said to have been introduced by Grimaldi, who would tap his nose and say, *C'est beaucoup*. In Australia it is a nickname for a man with only one eye.

Bolly: is a nickname given at Marlborough School to a fat boy. From steamed suet pudding which is, in shape, similar to a bolster. There may also be some connection with *boil*: the pudding is boiled, hence boiley, hence Bolly.

Bolsh(ie): nickname for any man who insists on boring his peers stiff by constant complaining against authority, and the established order of things: an agitator.

Bomb see *Fireworks*.

Bomb(er): not an explosive missile, but short for Bombardier, and an inseparable nickname of any man named Wells: from the name of the famous boxer, Bombardier Billy Wells, who was active in the early years of this century.

Bonce: a nickname used largely in London, for any person with a disproportionately large head.

Bones: a (now obsolete) nickname for a thin man.

Boney: is a nickname sometimes applied to a dealer in rags, bones and bottles, old iron and lumber. Probably more common in the Midlands and North, than in the South of England.

Bony Maroney see *Skinnigut*.

Bookworm see *Enos*.

Bool: is a Scottish nickname for a thickset man or boy. It is also used as a term of reference to a hard, worldly person. Probably a dialect shape of *Bull*.

Boots: is the time-honoured nickname of the porter and man-of-all-work at a small private (erstwhile 'Commercial') hotel. So named from his primal function of shining shoes while the wearers sleep. The modern chromium-plated caravansarai of the big city employs no one so friendly, human and helpful as the old-time *Boots*, and the shoes of the sleepless are buffed up by revolving brush and conveyor-belt technique. *Boots* could always play billiards, conveyor-belt operatives can not.

Bor: a term of address employed by fisherfolk of East Anglia. 'I don't like t'look o' the weather, bor': possibly from neighbour. It may be prefixed by the name—'Smith Bor' or 'Jones Bor'.

Bose see *Pipes*.

Bosseye: a general nickname for any person who squints: not from *boss*, the chief or leader, itself from Dutch *Baas*, master; but from dialect *boss*, crooked, one-sided, of little use, unreliable.

Boston: a Chinook Indian nickname for an American as distinct from an Englishman.

Botchky: is an American nickname for a Czech.

Bottomless: is an inseparable nickname (employed by 'educated' folk) for anyone named Pitt. It was the nickname of Wm. Pitt (1759–1806) and in his case may have had some reference to his very meagre build.

Bouncer: is a nickname for a big fleshy girl or woman. Used chiefly in Pennsylvania, but it has British currency also.

Bousy see *Blowze.*

Bowdykite: is a term of reference applied to a fat man. It is sometimes employed as a nickname.

Bowie: is the inevitable nickname of the youngest of three brothers at King Edward's School, Birmingham.

Bowney: is a nickname used in Suffolk for a fat person.

Bow-wow: is a nickname used in U.S.A. for a native of Boston.

Boy-in-blue see *Flatty.*

Boysie (Boyze): is a semiendearing nickname for a boy. Exclusive American, and confined in usage to Maryland. Its occasional use in England is in all cases individual—the term is independently 'invented' by the user. It has no general currency, although it qualifies as a general nickname.

Bozzer see *Flatty.*

Brain Basil see *Enos.*

Brains see *Enos.*

Brainy-pup see *Enos.*

Brassbonce see *Flatty.*

Brass hat: in military usage a General, or Staff Officer. The term ante-dates the XX C.: in naval usage an officer of Commander's rank or above. Derived from the gold lace decoration of caps and hats sacred to such exalted ranks.

Bratchet: is a nickname applied to a lively child. Used chiefly in Northumberland and Durham. Although it is, in this usage, an expression of affection (as *Imp* [q.v.] often is in the South of England), it may be reversed in its implication and used as a term of admonition. The word may also be spelt *Bratchart.*

Breakbones: a domestic servant's (hence, obsolete) nickname for a master or mistress of an exacting character.

Bricks: the inseparable nickname of any man named Morter. (This is a fairly common surname in Norfolk.) Often rendered 'Bricksan'. (Bricks and . . .).

Brigham: is the inseparable nickname of any man named Young. Its use appears to have origin in the Navy and from thence spread into civilian life. It is inclined to be abbreviated to Brig, Brigs, or Briggs From the name of the founder of the Mormon Sect.

Brilliant-bonce see *Enos*.

Brindy: is a nickname used chiefly in Derbyshire and Worcestershire, for a person with auburn hair.

Brockey see *Brokko*.

Brokko: nickname employed at sea for a messmate suffering from acne, or other facial spots. It is of Irish origin where it is inclined to take the form of *Brockey*, and to be applied to one with a pock-marked face.

Bronco: is the inseparable nickname of men named Rider.

Broomstick: is a nickname often given by Cockneys to a tall thin person.

Brother Jonathan: a now obsolescent nickname for the American nation, and a 'typical' American citizen: said to be formed on the name of Jonathan Trumbull, 1710–85, the friend of Washington, who so addressed him. See *Uncle Sam*.

Brum: is a general nickname for a man from Birmingham: from *Brumagem*, the local pronunciation, based on the 'shape' of the town's name in archaic English. Sometimes the word 'button' is added.

Brusey: is a nickname for an overgrown, tom-boyish girl. Cumberland dialect.

Bubbles: an inevitable nickname applied in youth to males who have the misfortune of possessing a florid fat face, a retroussé nose, a 'cupid's bow' mouth and fair curly hair. Later, when the chubby cheeks have degenerated into dewlaps and the curly head has become a bald pate, the nickname sticks. It is from an insipid child-portrait painted by Millais and purchased by Pears to advertise their excellent soap. This physical type is sometimes called *Pudd'n'ed* [q.v.] by Cockneys.

Buck: is the inseparable nickname of any man named Taylor. First used in the Army—probably cavalry—but general by the first decade of XX C. From the name of a spectacular horseman who performed in Buffalo Bill's team of Rodeo riders which visited England in 1889. In U.S.A. it is a general nickname for any young man, but particularly for a smart one, or one who considers himself smart.

Bucket: is a nickname likely to be given, in Cockney circles, to anyone named Powell. The name Powell, and the word 'pail', are indistinguishable one from the other hence, pail, a bucket.

Bucket-head: a German, but particularly a German soldier, from the shape of the steel helmet they favoured.

Bucket-maker: formerly a nickname used in U.S.A. for a native of Hingham, Mass.

Buckeye: is the nickname used in U.S.A. for a person from Ohio. From the *buckeye* tree (*Aesculus* *glabra*), indigenous horse-chestnut, the fruit of which resembles a deer's eye in appearance.

Buckra: is a nickname given by negroes to a white man. Recorded by Captain Marryat in *Peter Simple* (1834).

Buckskin: is an American nickname for a native of either Maryland or Virginia.

Bucky: is a nickname used in Scotland for a high-spirited boy, or for a tom-boyish girl.

Bud: nickname for one's personal (male) friend, and also a term of address to any stranger. Originally American, the expression has now a certain currency with the younger generation in England. It is also used in the sense 'Me an' 'im's buddies'. Bud from *brud*, itself shortened *brudder*, a slovenly pronunciation (or possibly foreign accent) of *brother*.

Buffalo: an American nickname for a native of North Carolina. From the naming of factions during the Civil War. The majority favoured the Union and were called the Buffaloes, the minority were the *Rumps*. It is also a general nickname used in U.S.A. for a fat woman.

Bug: is an Irish nickname for an Englishman. The Irish maintain that there were no bed-bugs in the country till Cromwell brought them over.

Bug-eaters: nickname of the inhabitants of Nebraska, U.S.A.

Bugs: a nickname applied in the Navy to any man who is dirty and untidy in his habits or dress.

Bulky: is a nickname used in Ireland for a policeman. Constables of the R.I.C. were usually big, corpulent—hence bulky—men.

Bull-lion: is a nickname that during the XIX Cent. was applied by Americans to an Englishman. It is a witty triple pun: 1. John *Bull*: 2. *Lion*, from the lions passant gardant in England's armorial insignia: 3. *Bullion*, from Britain's wealth in the XIX Cent. In this last respect the case is altered; and the term, had it not already been obsolete before 1914, would perforce have since become so.

Bumps see *Zambuk*.

Bun: is a nickname used in U.S.A. for a sponger: one who cannot be shaken off: from *bun*, a squirrel (which cannot be shaken off a tree) from Old English *bunn*, giving modern English bunny (rabbit).

Bungy: is the inseparable nickname of any man named Cooper, Cowper or Williams: used exclusively in the Navy—the last probably from some 'Jimmy Bungs' (cooper) named Williams. Beyond the confines of the Navy it is generally *Barney Williams*, which may be an altered form of *Bungy*.

Bunjie: Naval nickname for

the Instructor in Physical Training: from *bunjie*, slang for an india-rubber eraser, hence the india-rubber (flexible) man. It is also an inseparable nickname for any man named Edwards.

Bunnies: is the general nickname and term of reference for the population of Cedar Rapids: punning *see der rabbits*.

Bunny: is the inseparable nickname of any man named Warren. From Rabbit (bunny) warren, a numerous assembly of burrows. It is also the inseparable nickname of any man named Cross. From hot-cross bun.

Bunty: the inevitable nickname for a short, thick-set man. Late XIX C., probably from dialect *bunt*, short or thick, and influenced by *bunt*, the curvature of a sail full of wind. Current chiefly in the Navy and, to some extent, in the Army.

Burglar: is a nickname used during the 1914–18 war by British troops for a Bulgarian.

Burrer: a nickname used by costers for a member of their calling born in the Borough of Southwark—particularly if he is 'proud of it', and many, with justification, are.

Burrhead: one of the numerous American nicknames for a negro.

Bushey: is a frequently applied but not an inseparable nickname for any man named Fox: from the fox's bushy tail.

Busky: one of the nicknames that will be bestowed upon a man named Smith. Late XIX C. Naval and Military. There were probably so many Smiths that variants were essential.

Buster: is a general nickname for a boy in use throughout U.S.A., originally confined to Pennsylvania, but for a fat boy it has currency in Britain.

Busy-bee see *Flatty*.

Butch: is an American and Canadian nickname applied to any powerfully-built man or boy.

Butcher: is the inseparable nickname of any man named Lamb. It is frequently reduced to *Butch*, and it would be interesting to know whether what passes in Britain as an American masculine given name—Butch—is in fact merely a well-established nickname, and if so, whether its origin is identical.

Butter: is a schoolboy's nickname for one who is poor at ball games; from 'butter-fingers', one who lets a ball slip through.

Butterbox: is a nickname used in the Merchant Navy for a Dutchman. It is of American origin.

Butternut: is an American nickname for a native of Missouri. Formerly for a Confederate soldier. From the butter-nut tree from which brown dye is made.

Buttinski: (Mr. Mrs. or Miss) is an American nickname for one who rudely interrupts conversation, or who intrudes socially. From *Butt-in*, plus Polish suffix.

Butty: is a term of address used to a fellow-workman, a chance acquaintance or a familiar friend. It is, perhaps, employed more frequently in the North than in the South of England. It is possibly a dialect distortion, and

may ultimately come from *brother*.

Buzzard: is one of the nicknames applied in U.S.A. to persons from Georgia. (It is doubtless used with caution, since it is also a euphemism for 'bastard'—and some folk are sensitive.)

Byack: is a Scottish term of reference applied to a lazy, good-for-nothing person.

C

Cackey: is a nickname, now falling into obsolescence, for a left-handed person. The Education Authority's enlightened attitude to left-handedness has removed the slight stigma that it carried before mid-XX C. From cack-handed.

Cag: is a shortened and mutilated form of *cack*, see *Cackey*.

Cagian see *Acadian*.

Caikie see *Cakey*.

Cajon see *Acadian*.

Cakey: is a nickname given in Scotland and the North of England to one of inferior mental powers. Also spelt *caikie*.

Camp: is a nickname used in the Army for the Camp Commandant.

Canada: nickname bestowed upon any man (officer or rating) from Canada serving in the Royal Navy.

Cannacker see *Canuck*.

Canny: is a general nickname for a native of Newcastle. From

'canny Newcassel', the natives rather taking pride in their sharpness.

Canuck: a Canadian. Not used in England before the 1914–18 war, and never very popular. In use in Canada, and the U.S.A. at least as early as 1855. Probably originally from a native word meaning a French-Canadian, although in *Americanisms* (1877) by J. B. Bartlett, it is said to be an American-Irish corruption of *Connaught*.

Captain: is the inseparable nickname attached to Kettle or Kidd: from that of the famous Buccaneer. It is a frequent, but not an inseparable nickname of early XX Cent. fame. (The first Captain Kettle stores appeared in 1898.) It is also a familiar and complimentary term of address, used by Cockneys as a substitute for 'Guv'nor', when answering questions—for example, 'How do I get to . . .?' put to them by a 'proper gent': that is, one who is clearly not 'putting on the quiver', or acting in any way falsely, condescendingly, or 'superior like'.

Captain Blood: is a nickname given to 'nigger-driving' overseers in the docks. American usage.

Cargo: is a nickname given to R.N.V.R. officers serving with the Royal Navy. It is short for *Cargo-Bill*. (Many R.N.V.R. officers are Merchant Navy men.)

Carney: sailors' nickname for an officer who is a 'shore angel and ship's devil': one who is hard on the men when at sea, but in port (where his conduct can be observed) easy-going: from general slang, *carney*, cunning, false, hypocritical.

Carp(s): is the nickname given to the stage-carpenter. American 'show-business'.

Carrot-top see *Beetroot*.

Carrots: a rather juvenile, and 'better-class' term of reference to, and inevitable nickname for, one with auburn hair. It is sometimes converted to *Carroty*. 'Ayh say, Carroty, d'yah want to earn sixpence? Take this parcel for me then!'

Carroty-pow see *Beetroot*.

Cas: a term of reference to, formed on the initial letters of, Chief of Air Staff.

Cashy: is a nickname used in shops and cafés for the girl whose business is to occupy 'the desk'

and receive payments. Short form of *cashier*.

Cat: is the inevitable nickname of any man from Cheshire: sometimes *Moggy* [q.v.] and the shortened form, Mog.

Catawampus: is a temporary and friendly nickname that may be substituted for any other name on some specific occasions. It is chiefly American, but Dickens used it in *Martin Chuzzlewit*, hence it has a small currency in Britain. It is the name of a hobgoblin of the gremlin or jinx type.

Catlick: is a juvenile name for a Catholic. It has been common among schoolchildren since the beginning of the XX C., but it does not carry over into adulthood.

Cats: a nickname used in Ireland for the inhabitants of Kilkenny. Outside of Ireland 'Kilkenny cats' are assumed to be fighting felids.

Caustic: naval nickname for a grumbling, irritable, cantankerous hand.

Centennial: a general nickname used in U.S.A. for anyone from Colorado.

Chalky: is an alternative for *Blanco* [q.v.] inseparable nickname of any man named White. Whereas 'Blanco' is of military origin and usage, 'Chalky' is naval. Both are extended into civilian life.

Charley: is the inseparable nickname of any man named

Beresford: from Admiral Lord Charles Beresford, author of *Nelson and his Times*. It is also attached to any man named Noble, and (by contrast), to any man named Peace, from that picturesque character, Charlie Peace of Peckham, the master-cracksman of the XIX C. It is also the inseparable nickname of any man named Wagg: from to *Charlie Wag*, play truant. Recorded by Charles Hindley, 1867. Up to *c.* 1914, the specifically Cockney form was, 'to hop the wag'. It was, too, the nickname of the London night watchman, who preceded Sir Robert Peel's Police Force. The watchman's nickname was derived from King Charles I who, *c.* 1640, set up the Watch in order to suppress street offences. In the R.A.F. it is a term of reference and nickname for the Commanding Officer, for whom it is sometimes extended to *Charley Orange*.

Chatham Rats: a collective nickname for naval ratings of the Chatham Division.

Chats: is an alternative nickname for a man named Harris. 'Chats' are lice: possibly from *chattels* (itself related to *cattle*, i.e. property) which bolsters up the seamen's Lodging House keeper theory expressed under *Bogey* [q.v.].

Chatty: is the inseparable nickname of any man named Mather. Mathering, or mauthering, is, in Northern dialect, talking (chatting) excessively.

Chaw: is one of the nicknames given to Irishmen in America.

Chef: nickname bestowed upon the ship's cook, and the worse his cooking, the more certain the name.

Chemist, The: naval nickname for the ship's medical officer.

Cherry: a nickname applied to a girl or young woman. Its use was confined to the American underworld in XIX Cent., but it climbed the social scale, and may now be regarded as a standard given name.

Chesky: is an American nickname for a Czech.

Chicagorillas: is the general nickname used in America for natives or inhabitants of Chicago.

Chick-a-biddy: see *Biddy*.

Chico: is an American nickname for a Filipino.

Chief: term of address used in the Navy for the Senior Engineer Officer: also for a Chief Petty Officer, the latter sometimes being distinguished by *Chiefy*.

Chief housemaid: a naval term of reference to the First Lieutenant, who is responsible for the general cleanliness of the ship.

Chim: is the Scottish shape of *Chum* [q.v.].

Chinamang: an American nickname for a Chinaman. The addition of the final 'g' gives a Chinese flavour to the word.

China-bird see next entry.

Chinky: nickname for any sailor who, having served in the good old days on 'China Side', is inclined to tell his tales too often. From *Chink* a Chinaman, originally Australian slang. *China bird* is sometimes employed as a term of reference.

Chippa: one of the inseparable nicknames of men named Wood(s).

Chips: naval nickname for a ship's carpenter (or a shipwright). In the third person he is referred to as 'the Chippy-chap'. Altered to *Chippy*, it is the inseparable nickname of any man named Carpenter; more common in the Army than in the Navy.

Chisel: nickname bestowed upon any man with a prominent chin. Services and civilian.

Choco: is the Army's nickname for those conscientious objectors who, having failed to tell the correct story, were conscripted. They were not asked to carry anything so nasty as a rifle, but were permitted to spend their time usefully employed in the sanitary squad carrying latrine buckets. *Choco* is short for chocolate, but not connected with the next entry. [Note: Everybody, including the troops, had respect for a genuine conscientious objector—such, for example, as a member of The Society of Friends (Quakers). Those who objected to hurting other men frequently volunteered for ambulance or other non-combatant work. Those whose objections were to being themselves hurt, became the Chocos.]

Chocolate (pronounce Choclit): generally reduced to *chokker*, or to *chokko*, is the inseparable nickname of any man named Brown. It is also a friendly nickname for any 'coloured' man, and particularly if he is either a boxer or a wrestler.

Choctaw: is an American nickname for a Spaniard.

Chokker (or **Chokko**) see *Chocolate*.

Chopback: is a nickname for a Hastings fisherman. According to Frank Bowen, it refers to an incident in a fight with some Dutch traders.

Chow: general nickname for a Chinaman. Exclusively Australian in usage. Probably from the *Chow* element that occurs in the name of numerous Chinese dishes. Chinese Restaurants seem to be more commonly patronized in Australia than they are in England. It has also a rhyming element: Chow—*cow*: the latter, a term of contempt for a person of either sex, or for the inanimate, in Australia.

Chowder (short form of *Chowderhead*): is an American nickname for a stupid person.

Christmas: Father see *Father*.

Chub(b): is a nickname used in U.S.A. for natives of, or inhabitants of, Texas.

Chubby: see *Jumbo*.

Chuck: is a nickname that, in the event of a man's surname attracting an 'inseparable', may be given to any man whose personal name is Charles. [Certain other given names are subject to juvenile rhymes, which do not qualify as nicknames.] See I. and P. Opie, *The Lore and Language of Schoolchildren* (1959).

Chucks: nickname for the bo'sun in the old navy, now obsolescent. It was sometimes rendered 'Mr. Chucks'. See Captain Marryatt, *Midshipman Easy* (1836).

Chum: is a term of address and a nickname used in a friendly spirit to anyone, especially a crony. It was overworked during the 1914–18 war, but its use is now slightly old-fashioned. Partridge says: 'First recorded in 1684 —Creech's dedication, "To my chum Mr. Hodley of Wadham College." This term seems at first to have been University s[lang]. . . . Perhaps by abbreviation and collision of *chamberfellow* and *mate*.' See his *Dictionary of Slang*. . . . p. 154.

Chunka: is one of the inseparable nicknames of any man named Wood(s).

Chunky: is a general nickname for a short, thick-set man. From *chunk*, a thick, bulky piece. Recorded in Ray's *Country Words* (1691).

Cigs: is the term of reference by which—during the Second

War—the Chief of the Imperial General Staff was indicated.

Clam catchers: one of the nicknames bestowed upon the inhabitants of New Jersey, U.S.A.

Clam-humpers: nickname applied to inhabitants of Maryland, U.S.A.

Clampy: is the inevitable nickname of a flatfooted, or heavy treading man in the Navy: from Clamping, coming down heavily on.

Clay-eater: is a nickname used in U.S.A. for natives of South Carolina or of Georgia. It is also applied to a farm-hand from the deep South.

Clever Dick see *Enos*.

Cleverguts see *Enos*.

Cleverpot see *Enos*.

Cleversides see *Enos*.

Cleversticks see *Enos*.

Clift: is a term of reference used in Ireland for one who is accepted as a fool by strangers, but as a rogue by his neighbours. The same idea is expressed by Cockneys in the phrase 'more R than F'.

Clina: nickname for a girl: generally one met casually as, for example, at a dance hall. The term is used to some extent by Cockneys, but is favoured by Cockney Jews: from *Klein*, German for 'small' hence 'little one'. In the early XX C. it had currency in Australia.

Clink: is in Lincolnshire dialect a term of reference to, and a nickname for, a tale-bearing, mischief-making woman. From *Clink*, the imitative sound of metal being struck. Sometimes extended to *Clinky*.

Clipper: a dialect nickname, used in various parts of Ireland, Scotland and England, for a mean, close-fisted person—one who clips, cuts, or reduces his workmen's pay if they lose a minute of time.

Clippy: is a nickname for a female bus-conductor. A formation on *Nippy* [q.v.] but of newspaper usage only—the term never 'caught on', and all endeavours to popularize it have now been abandoned.

Clootey: is an Irish nickname for a left-handed person.

Closh: a general nickname, and a term of reference, used in the Navy for any Essex-born member of the crew. From Klaus (or Klaas) short form of Nicholas, a common Dutch given name: there is a strong strain of Dutch blood in Essex. Colchester has some old Dutch architecture, and much reclaimed coastal land is in the form of Dutch Islands. *Mynheer Closh* is an American nickname for a Dutchman.

Cloudy (or **Cloudy Joe**): is a Services (R.A.F. and Navy) nickname for the Meteorological Officer.

Clubs: a Naval nickname for an instructor in Physical Training. In the Navy, Indian club and dumb-bell exercises are more popular than Swedish drill.

Cluck: is a term of reference to, and a nickname for, a stupid person. The use is confined to U.S.A.

Clutterbuck (or **Mr. Clutterbuck**): is a nickname given to a bulky, bovine slow-moving person who habitually disposes himself so as to cause an obstruction. From *Clutter*, to litter, to make untidy.

Coaly: general nickname for an itinerant vendor of coals, now obsolescent on account of 'clean-air' movements, and the popularization of oil-fuel for domestic heating as well as in the increase in blocks of flats with central heating (oil-fuelled very often).

Cobber: nickname for one's companion whether his own name is known or not. General term for an acquaintance. Australian in origin, and mainly in usage, but it has some currency in England.

Cock: a friendly form of Cockney address to any man or boy, known or unknown. The term has its origin in cock fighting—cock o' the pit, the winner: cock o' the walk, hence a plucky fighter, hence one deserving of admiration, hence 'Cock' or 'Old Cock' is not merely friendly but is complimentary. The world 'old' may be attached even when addressing a young boy; it is merely an emphasis. Sometimes it is given a final 'er' *Cocker*, which is about one hundred years old, and is from Standard English, a supporter of cock fighting, nevertheless, modern youth believes that *Cocker* is an importation from U.S.A. It is also the inseparable nickname of any man named Robin, Robins, or Robinson. From the rhyme, 'Who killed Cock Robin?'

Cock-eye: is an alternative form of *Boss-eye* [q.v.].

Cockalorum: is a general friendly term of address which, in the XX Cent. is losing the inference of inferiority that it carried previously. It is now used simply as an extension of *Cock* [q.v.] but is more inclined to be applied to a young than to an elderly person.

Cockney: is the inevitable nickname of any Londoner who happens to be serving in a provincial, particularly North of England, regiment, or who is one among a number of men of mixed provincial origins in a specialist corps as, for example, the Royal Engineers.

Codder (shortened from Cape Codder): is an American nickname for one from Cape Cod.

Coffee: is a nickname for a negro which seems to be both self-inflicted and ostentatious. It is used for (and by) coloured men who live by showmanship, either on the stage or as market-salesmen. It may, however, be of a less obvious origin than superficially appears. *Cuffy* or *Kofi*, is a native African word (Ghana) meaning 'one born upon Friday', and is used as a given name for a male child born on that day.

Coksey: is a Scottish and North of England dialect nickname for a conceited, arrogant person. Also spelt *Coxy*.

Colleen: a general nickname for an Irish girl.

College-John: is the nickname for the Porter at Westminster School.

Colonel: a general nickname which may be applied to anyone. It is employed by both the Cockneys and the Bowery boys, but in London it is merely friendly and familiar, in New York it is complimentary and flattering; further, it is used over a wider social cross-section in America than in England where anyone who would not use the term *Guv'nor* [q.v.] would not call a person Colonel. It is also applied, in the States, to anyone from Kentucky.

Commie: nickname for members of the Communist Party; or (the majority) those who pretend to be; or, very commonly, those who condemn the Government, the Social System and all forms of authority but do not support anything—not even themselves.

Conk(e)y: as a nickname for anyone with a strongly marked 'Roman' nose ante-dates 1815 (see Partridge, *Dictionary of Slang*) but at that period it was applied to the Duke of Wellington and has since become popular at many social levels. *Conk*, the nose, is probably from conch(shell). I. and P. Opie, in *The Lore amd Language of Schoolchildren* (1959) say: 'There are also, according to juvenile observers, people with "ferret-noses", "pig-noses", "jelly noses", "long cucumber-noses", "Peggy Parrot noses", "cheese-cutters", and "Rudolphs", [q.v.].' To this list might be added 'Titty noses' and 'Toffee noses'.

Connie: is the inevitable nick-name of any man notoriously suffering from constipation as a chronic condition.

Coof: is a term of reference used by natives of Nantucket for a native of Cape Cod, and for anyone not a native of Nantucket.

Cookie: naval term of address to the ship's cook if he is not bad enough to enjoy the title *Chef* [q.v.]. It is used at all social levels in civilian life, but may have originated afloat.

Coon: is an American nick-name for a negro. Current chiefly in the Southern States. Probably from *Racoon*, as some other slang and colloquial terms are.

Coosie: is a general nickname for a cook, particularly for a Chinese cook. Of American origin, but gradually becoming naturalized British: at present underworld use only.

Copper: nickname for a Police Constable, from his mandate to 'cop', catch, arrest a miscreant. The term was originally theatrical, but is now universal. In the U.S.A. *Cop* is its abbreviated form.

Copper belly: a term of reference, not of address, to a man with abdominal localized fat. The 'copper' is not, in this setting, connected with either the yellow metal, or the policeman, but with the cauldron mounted in a fireplace which in the early XX C. was a feature of most Cockney homes. Washing is now performed by electrical mach-inery.

Copper-crust see *Beetroot*.

Copper knob: this term, gene-rally reduced to 'Copper', is one of several that is bestowed upon any person, of either sex, having auburn hair. It is more likely to be heard in the Ward Room than on the lower deck, both in, and out of, the Navy.

Cordite Jaunty: term of re-ference to the Chief Gunner's Mate in the Naval School of Gunnery.

Corncracker: a general nick-name used in U.S.A. for anyone from Kentucky.

Cornstalk: is a nickname often given to a tall man. Originally (early XIX C.) a New South Wales, and later (mid-XIX C.) any Australian citizen.

Corp: a friendly term of address for a Corporal. Its use in the Army is as old as the rank.

Cosher: is the inseparable nickname of any man named Hinds (or Hynds), probably having reference to some formerly notorious bluejacket who was handy (or too handy) with a 'cosh' (bludgeon). The following seems too elaborate a theory of origin: *Cosher*, from Yiddish (or Hebrew) *Kasha(er)* i.e. clean, lawful, edible, not at variance with food tabu. The rump of a beast, *hind* quarters, carrying a network of undrainable blood-vessels, is not Kasha, hence, by inversion, '*Kasha Hinds*'.

Cosie: is the general nickname of any girl named Kathleen. Chiefly of Irish usage.

Cotton: is a Pennsylvanian nickname for 'an old man with young ideas'. Perhaps with reference to the white hair of venerable age, and to reveal that in this particular individual it has been dyed.

Cousin: 'A familiar epithet or term of address,' says Wright, and gives combinations: '(1) *Cousin Betty*, a harmless madwoman, a vagrant, beggar; (2) — *Jack*, a Cornishman; (3) — *Jacky*, a term of contempt, a fool, a coward; (4) — *Tommy*, a harmless madman, a vagrant, beggar.'

Cousin Jacky (or **Jan**) see *Jan*.

Covess-dinge: is a mid-XIX C. American underworld nickname for a coloured prostitute.

Cowstail see *Muttoned*.

Coxy see *Coksey*.

Crabby: a nickname thrust upon any person of an irritable and complaining nature. It is chiefly Cockney in usage, and is employed largely by boys whose noisy games are interrupted by such a one. Before 1914 it was often employed as a taunt to be shouted after the person when in the street.

Cracker: a general nickname used in U.S.A. for anyone from either Georgia, or Florida.

Cranky: is a nickname sometimes given to a person who has strange ideas, or a monomania. From *crank*, bent.

Crapaud: is an American nickname for a Frenchman. From Old French, *crapaud*, a toad.

Craterface see *Zambuk*.

Crawley or **Creepy:** are both nicknames of equal weight value and meaning, either of which will be given to a sychophant.

Creepy see *Crawley*.

Creepy-crawler see *Muttoned*.

Creoles: nickname applied to the inhabitants of Louisiana, U.S.A. In Britain the word is popularly supposed to apply to one of mixed negro and Caucasian race; however, in the West Indies, men of all races, horses, cattle and sheep are, if native, described as Creole. In the Southern States of America the word is never applied to a negro or one of mixed race: in Louisville, and in

New Orleans, it is applied only to a person of French antecedents. The word is from Spanish *criollo*, one born in the West Indies, or the U.S.A.

Cribby: nickname for any man who is a notorious maker of complaints. Used in both the Navy and the Army but probably originating in the latter, particularly the cavalry: from *crib-biter*, a horse that 'complains' by biting his crib.

Crippen: a nickname often given to a person, of wild, unkempt appearance. From the name of Dr. H. H. *Crippen*, the sensational murderer (1910). Much publicity was gained by Captain Kendall, of *The Montrose*, sending a message on 22 July, by *wireless* telegraphy.

Croaky: is a nickname given to one who has a gruff voice.

Crocus: is a nickname given to a quack-doctor by other market-spielers. Probably a pun on *croak*, to kill, *us*.

Crook-catcher see *Flatty*.

Crootles: is a Scottish and North of England dialect nickname for a person with disproportionately short legs.

Croppy (or **Croppy boy**): is an old (? XVIII Cent.) nickname for a militant rebel in Ireland. From their cropped hair.

Crosspatch: is a general nickname for a disagreeable person.

Crouly: is a nickname given in Ireland to an undersized person.

From a local name for the smallest in a litter of pigs. Cf. *titman*.

Crow (short for **Jim Crow**): is an American nickname for a negro. Originally English dialect for a street-performer, a busker.

Crowpoo: is a seaman's nickname for a Frenchman. From *crapaud*, 'a frog', hence, a version of *Froggy* [q.v.].

Crowthumper: is one of the nicknames given in U.S.A. to a native, or an inhabitant, of Maryland.

Crumb: is a contemptuous nickname given to an insignificant person: it appears to be an importation from U.S.A.

Crutchy: is a North of England nickname for one who habitually walks with the aid of a crutch: a cripple.

Crystal Jellybottom see *Jumbo*.

Cuddy: is an American nickname for a negro. It was also a nickname used throughout the old Navy for Admiral Collingwood.

Cuffy see *Coffee*.

Cully: a term of address to one's friend or close companion, but extended in use as a friendly term of address to a semi- or a complete stranger. The word is old established Cockney, and has experienced several changes in meaning: early XVII Cent. a fool; later, and in XVIII Cent., a Constable; late XVIII Cent., any man; XIX Cent., one's friend; and mid-XX Cent. obsolescent. Its possible origin is from Culls, and abbreviation of Cullions, the testicles.

C——-face: is an even more friendly form of address than is *shit-face* [q.v.].

Curly: humour by inversion is a characteristic of slang. *Curly* is the nickname of a bald-headed man. In general use: naval in origin.

Cut-throats: one of the nicknames of the inhabitants of Idaho, U.S.A.

Cutemup: is a nickname given in the American underworld to a doctor. *Cut 'em up.*

Cuts: is a nickname used in the Navy for any man who earns the reputation of a humorist.

D

Dab toe: a nickname given by stokers in the Navy to seamen.

Dad: a friendly nickname for any elderly man: even a total stranger will be so addressed by a Cockney.

Daddy see *Pa*.

Daddy-longlegs see *Skinnigut*.

Dago: a nickname, originally naval, but now universal, bestowed on 'swarthy' foreigners. Strictly it belongs only to Spanish and Portuguese seamen (from *Diego*, a given name), but the extension of its use to civilians has also extended its geographical fittingness. Its employment by the general public is far greater in U.S.A. than in Britain. It has been in use more than a hundred years.

Dairy Dot: was the nickname used during the Second War for female milk-round workers.

Daisy: is the inseparable nickname of any man named Dean. It might be a confusion between *Nellie* [q.v.] from the song 'Nellie Dean' and *Daisy* (of the bicycle built for two) influenced by alliteration; but it is also the inseparable of men named Bell— for the belle of the bicycle was so named.

Damn Yankee: is a term of reference used in the Southern States of U.S.A., for anyone from Iowa—or any other Northern State. Stripped of the adjective, the term Yank(y) [q.v.] has a different flavour. There is a story told that Dr. Herman Adler, the English 'Chief Rabbi', when addressing a meeting of Jews said: 'There are two congregations. Jews and Bloody Jews—to which do you, personally, belong?'

Dan: is the inseparable nickname of any man named Tucker: from the refrain of a negro song,

Out ob de way ol' Dan Tucker.

The reference is to Captain Daniel Tucker, second Governor of Bermuda. It is also the inseparable nickname of any man named Cole(s). See also *Knobby*. In the first decade of XX C. it was a general nickname for the attendant in a public lavatory from a vulgar song beginning:

Dan, Dan, Dan,
The Lava-tory man,
Underneath the ground all day:
Buying ha'penny Finals,[1]
Cleaning out u-ri-nals . . .

Dandy: is the inseparable nickname of any man named Evans. Of naval origin and usage.

Dandyprat: 'a little funny fellow'. *The Universal Etymological Dictionary*, 3 edn. Nathaniel Bailey, 1737.

Dansker: nickname given in the Merchant Navy to any Danish seaman.

Dap: is a term of reference used by negroes, for a white man. Its use, which is confined to U.S.A., is restricted to educated negroes.

Dark meat: is a term of reference to a coloured prostitute, or to any attractive coloured woman. In use in Britain since *c.* 1950, but of American origin.

Darky: is a very common, but not inseparable, nickname for a man named Smith. It has no reference to personal appearance—a blond, or a redheaded Smith

may be called Darkie. It is evolved out of *blacksmith*, and by inversion is sometimes applied to men named White. It is also a very common general nickname for a negro.

David: is (in the Navy) the inseparable nickname of any man named Beatty: from Admiral Sir David (afterwards Earl) Beatty. The use of his given name as a term of reference to him was common to all ranks before the Battle of Jutland. After that engagement it was converted into an 'inseparable' for all Beattys. (Earl Beatty died 1936).

Deak see *Deke*.

Dee-donk: is an alternative spelling of *Didonck* [q.v.].

Deke: is an American university nickname for a member of the *Delta Kappa Epsilon* fraternity. Also spelt *Deak*.

Dekker(a): is the inseparable nickname of any boy named Derek (or Derrick). Evolved since the Second War, it remains to be seen whether it will grow up with its owner.

Demo see *Jimmo*.

Derzy: a military nickname for the Regimental Tailor, from Hindustani *dhirzi*, a tailor.

Dick (sometimes **Dicky**): is the inseparable nickname of any man named Richards. It may have been influenced by the naval *King Dick*, Admiral Sir Frederick Richards, First Sea Lord during the 1890's.

---

[1] Sporting editions of newspapers containing the latest betting news.

Dick Smith: is a nickname given to any unsociable, morose member of a baseball team.

Dicky: is the inseparable nickname of any man named Bird. From the infantile *dicky-bird* for any bird. There is, too, *pussy cat* but, strangely, nothing to precede 'dog', 'bow-wow' being used instead.

Dicky (the first): a Royal Navy term of reference applied to the First Lieutenant. It is also a general nickname, used particularly in the Navy, for anyone serving in an 'acting' capacity for the duration of such service. It seems to come from the world of Law: a clerk, acting for a solicitor, is his Dicky.

Dicky Dyke: is a nickname for a lavatory attendant. Its use seems to be peculiar to 'public school types'.

Dicky-Sam: is a general nickname for any native of Liverpool: probably from dialect usage.

Diddle-diddle-dumpling see *Jumbo.*

Didonck (or Dee-donc): was a nickname applied to any Frenchman at the time of the Crimean War: from *dis donc.*

Dig: is a shortened form of the next entry.

Digger: a friendly term of address to, or description of, any Australian or New Zealander. During the 1914–18 war men from the Antipodes used it to address each other, and 'the troops', particularly Cockneys, took to it so kindly that it was extended to include any of one's comrades irrespective of place of origin. It was retained in postwar civilian life, and it may sometimes be heard even today. Its present use, though by no means universal, is not necessarily confined to 'old sweats'.

Dilly-day-dream see *Muttoned.*

Dimmo see *Jimmo.*

Dimples see *Zambuk.*

Ding: is a nickname given to an Italian by an Australian. Since *c.* 1920, but of unknown origin.

Dingbat: is a nickname used in U.S.A. for various foreigners, but chiefly for Italians and Chinamen.

Ding-dong: is the inseparable nickname of any man named Bell. It occurs (with explanation) in *Gently Dust the Corpse* (1960), S. H. Courtier's Australian thriller. Sometimes shortened to *Dinger.*

Dinge (or **Dingey**): is a general nickname used in U.S.A. for any negro, but particularly for a child. The term is more than a century old, and still has restricted currency.

Dinger see *Ding-dong.*

Dinghy: the inseparable nickname of any man named Reed, Reid, or Read. A dinghy is a small row-boat, hence the combination may be influenced by 'Reeds', a dialect word meaning fishing from a small boat.

Dink: is a nickname for a Chinaman. Used by Australians, formed on *Chink*.

Dinkus see *Waynam*.

Dinty: is an inseparable nickname for any man named Moor, or Moore, or Muir.

Dixie: is the inseparable nickname for a man named Dean. From a former popular footballer.

Dizzy: a middle-class term of reference (now obsolescent) to a particularly clever man: from the name of Benjamin Disraeli, First Lord Beaconsfield.

Doc: Mencken, *American Language*, says, 'When I was a boy in Baltimore, *c.* 1890, every youngster whose father was a physician was called *Doc*, and any boy whose father had any other title got it likewise.'

Doctor: is the general nickname bestowed upon a ship's cook in the American Merchant Service.

Dodger: the punning inseparable nickname of any man named Long. In the unlikely event of the reader being unable to see the point, he is advised to dodge along to *Jumper* and study that entry. It is also the inseparable nickname of any man named Green. To 'act green' is to pretend to stupidity: this pretence leads to mess-deck sweeping instead of more strenuous duties: a mess-deck sweeper is a 'dodger'.

Doggo: is the nickname for a gruff, tough, not-too-fond-of-his-face sort of sailor: 'beautiful as a bull-dog'. Almost (but not quite) an alternative term is *Ratto*: but whereas Doggo is broad-faced and heavy jowled, Ratto is sharp of features.

Dolly: the inseparable nickname of any man named Gray (Grey): from the late-Victorian music-hall song 'Good-bye Dolly Grey'. Of naval origin, its usage is extended into civilian life.

Dolly-Mixture see *Midge*.

Dolly Mopp: is a sailor's nickname for a landlady of a private house who 'lets' to seamen. *Dolly Mopp's Garrett* is any privately-owned lodging house for sailors. It is also a general nickname for an overdressed woman. Popular in late XIX C. when it implied a servant girl in her mistress's gown. Now extinct: there are no servant girls, and the tendency is for women to *under*dress.

Dolly Varden: is the nickname given aboard ship to any man who is too 'nice' in his manners, and too prim in personal appearance. It is not exactly a compliment, being intended to imply effeminacy.

Domino: is an American nickname for any negro, but particularly for one with strong white teeth.

Don: is a nickname for a Spaniard. Now obsolete in England, but still employed in the U.S.A. From the Spanish title.

Dotty: is a general nickname given to a native of Derbyshire.

Doughboy: a nickname chosen by the American troops, during the 1914–18 war, for themselves. The British public was advised by the Press not to call them 'Yanks', because, they alleged, Americans considered it offensive. (They did not, and they do not.) The British Press went a step further and invented 'Sammies' [q.v.]—to which the Americans did object. 'Dough-boys' was first used by Federal troops *c.* 1862, from their large dumpling-like, globular tunic buttons, or, according to some accounts, earlier, *c.* 1846, during the Mexican campaign, from adobe huts in which U.S. infantry was quartered.

Doughcock: is a nickname used in the Navy for a man who is genuinely slow-witted. It is derived from West Country dialect. In its reduced form, *Doughy*, it refers to general foolishness, but is not a nickname: 'No use to ask him to help with the job— you know he's doughy.'

Doughy: is the inseparable nickname of any man named Baker. Clearly an occupational nickname.

Draftie: is the nickname for the Drafting Commander at a Naval Depot.

Drafting Jaunty: Drafting Master-at-Arms in a Naval Barracks.

Drainings: a now obsolescent nickname used for the ship's cook.

Drainpipe: is a nickname bestowed upon a tall thin man.

Drains: is the general nickname of a Sanitary Officer, under Colonial Administration.

Drawers: is the inseparable nickname of any man named Chester. From a play upon chest-of-drawers.

Dripper: is a nickname used in the Navy, since *c.* 1930, for a confirmed bore and grouser. From *drip*, nonsense: allied to *drivel*.

Duck (or **Ducks** or **Ducky**): is the inseparable nickname of any man named Drake, also of any man named Mallard. It may also be given to a short man—from Duck's disease (i.e. arse too near the ground); and it is the nickname given to the Matron at Felstead School.

Duff Chokers: Lowestoft fishermen's term of reference for men from Yarmouth.

Duffer: is a dialect nickname for a tallyman who deals mainly in women's clothes.

Duffo: is the nickname of any member of the crew of a ship out of Devonport. From *duff*, boiled suet pudding, said, by ratings of Portsmouth and Chatham ships, to be the natural food of a West Countryman.

Duke: is the inseparable nickname of any man named Kent. Since *c.* 1930, but in XIX C. it was an inevitable nickname for any man with a prominent nose, and the reference was to the Duke of Wellington. In the latter sense it is recorded by D. W. Barrett, *Life Among the Navvies*, 1880.

Dumb-bell: is a general nickname for any deaf mute: often reduced to *Dumbo*.

Dummy: is the inseparable nickname of any man in the Navy named Oliver: from Admiral of the Fleet Sir Henry Oliver, who said little but thought much. At the time of writing (spring 1960) he is still with us, aged 97. In civilian life it is the inevitable nickname by which any deaf mute is known: from *dumb*.

Dumpling: is a general nickname for natives or inhabitants of Norfolk: from the county custom of eating suet dumpling soaked in gravy before dinner: *Norfolk dumpling*.

Dumpy: is a dialect nickname for a thick-set person.

Dunderclug: is a Scottish nickname for a Dutchman. From a dialect form of *thunder clogs*, noisy (because wooden) shoes.

Dustbin (sometimes **Dustole**): is a nickname favoured by Cockneys: it is forged within the family as a rule, but becomes general in usage. Applied to the one with a good appetite who will invariably eat what the others leave.

Dusty: a form of address employed by Cockneys to the Corporation dustmen, or, to be up-to-date, the Municipal Refuse Collection Operative. It is also the nickname given to a ship's assistant-steward being, in that setting, a shortened form of *Dusty boy*.

Dusty: inseparable nickname of any man named Miller. A miller, during his working hours, was always covered from head to foot with a sprinkling of very fine white dust (in the modern mill this condition of labour does not exist), hence the nickname arises from the trade, and is transposed into the surname. Its extension to *Rhodes* may have been earlier than the first decade of the XX C. but at that time it became popularized as the new motor traffic emphasized the unsuitability of the old horse roads. The pun on Roads and Rhodes is obvious. Occasionally *Dusty Smith*, from the shower of ashes that was a feature of a hand-blown forge: also *Dusty Jordan*.

Dutcher: is an American nickname for either a Dutchman or a German.

Dutchy: is the inseparable nickname of any man named Holland. In writing the origin is clear, but when spoken there is room for a misunderstanding: 'But why Dutchy? Holland is a kingdom.' It is also the nickname, generally friendly, bestowed upon Dutch, German and Scandinavian hands in the Merchant Navy, and to those who receive it, the name sticks when they come ashore and settle down. The standard English word 'Dutchman' referred, in the XVIII C., to a native of Germany: one from Holland was a 'Hollander'. It is also likely to be given to a short, thick-set man, particularly such a one having disproportionately broad buttocks. (A woman of such a figure is described as 'broad in the beam as a Dutch barge'. It is also applied as a nickname for a bald-headed man, enlikening the head to a Dutch cheese.

Dyno (or **Dino**): originally a miner's nickname for one who worked with dynamite, but now applied to a Mexican labourer. Its use is confined to railway-track workers in U.S.A.

E

Eagle-beak: is an American nickname for a Jew. Wentworth and Flexner define the term in their *Dictionary of American Slang* (1960) and date it, by quotation, 1939.

Ebony: is a general nickname for a negro. American in origin, and still in frequent use there. Popular in England during the XIX Cent. but now seldom heard. From the black wood of *Diospyros Ebonus*.

Eddiwop: is a Cockney nickname for anyone with an abnormally big head. It is a telescoped and reversed form of 'whopping (i.e. big) head'.

Eddy: was a nickname used in the R.A.F. for the man on sanitary fatigue. Eric Partridge gives in the *Supplement* to *Dictionary of Slang* . . . (6th edn.) 'Elsan Eddy (Loosely Eddie). A latrine-cleaner ("sanitary wallah")

. . . ob[solescent] by 1950, [obsolete] by 1955. A blend of *Elsan*, a proprietary name, and, by a pun, *Nelson Eddy*, the famous singer.'

Edge: is a term of reference to the Adjutant. It is a Cockney (and therefore contagious!) form of *Adj*, merely the shortened form.

Edna: inseparable nickname for any man named May: from Edna May, the famous theatrical 'Star', fl 1890–1900.

Eel: is an American nickname for a native of New England.

Egg (**Eggy** or **Eggo**): is a friendly and chaffing nickname for a bald-headed man. Chiefly of naval, but also of some civilian use. It is also a nickname given to a coward. Sometimes changed to *Yolky*. Both refer to Yellow.

Egyptian: is an American

nickname for a native of Southern Illinois.

Eightball: is a nickname given in U.S.A. to a negro. Wentworth and Flexner (1960) explain: 'because the No. 8 ball in the game of pool is coloured solid black.'

Eli: a nickname given in the U.S.A. to any student or postgraduate of Yale University. From Elihu Yale (1648–1721).

Engines: is the nickname by which the Engineer, or Technical, Officer is known. R.A.F. usage since *c*. 1925.

Enoch: is a nickname given to an ugly man: from a radio character. According to I. and P. Opie, it is interchangeable with *Goofy*, another (?) character in the same radio-feature, 'Happidrome' (*c*. 1940).

Enos: is a nickname bestowed upon a person who either possesses or pretends to superior knowledge. From the name of a brand of health-salts, punning '*he knows*'. It may be used either in admiration or derision. I. and P. Opie found that children 'show for the bright boy or girl both admiration and contempt. They are willing to acclaim anyone who habitually comes top of the class without apparent effort, naming him Genius, The Brains, Miracle Man, Professor [q.v.], and Topper; but they look down upon the one who has to work hard to keep first place. Such a person is a Swotter, Swotpot, or

Stewpot. . . . People who keep at their work are Ants, Bookworms, Slaves, Plodderoners, Old Grindstones. A clever boy is most often styled Clever Dick or, less frequently, Brainy-pup, Brilliant-bonce, Cleverguts, Cleverpot, Cleversides, Cleversticks, Jingler, Know-all, Squelch, and (in Oxford) Brain Basil—all terms which may also, on occasions, be ironical, meaning that he is: artful, over-witty, too clever by half, a show-off, a snob, or a poshy guy.' See *Lore and Language of Schoolchildren* (1959) pp. 178–9.

Enzedder: an Australian term of reference to any man from New Zealand. Derived from the initials N.Z. Also *Maorilander*. Both recorded by Sidney J. Baker in *The Drum*, 1959.

Epsom: is the inseparable nickname of any man named Salt.

'Erringut (Herring-gut): is a Cockney nickname for a thin man.

Equality Jack: was a disrespectful nickname used in the old Navy for any two-faced officer who tried to win favour by being familiar with ratings.

'Erb (Herbert): a term of address to any member of the Royal Air Force. The names 'George' and 'Jack' were also employed, but neither of them were comparable in popularity. 'A reg'lar 'Erb!' refers to a humorist, in which usage it is a descriptive title, not a nickname, and its use is not restricted to the R.A.F.

Eska: the inseparable nickname of any man in the Army named Moffatt: from the Arabic.

Everest: is a nickname for a tall, weedy boy. Recorded by I. and P. Opie in *Lore and Language of Schoolchildren* (1959) who point out that its use does not ante-date the ascent.

Eye on see *Iron.*

F

Face: is a Cockney nickname for any man whose face is considered noteworthy: curious, but neither ugly nor notably good-looking. In use before 1910, and still common. In U.S.A. it is a negro's nickname for a white man.

Face-packer see *Hungry-guts.*

Fadge or **Fadgy:** is a North of England dialect nickname for a thick-set, or corpulent, person of either sex.

Fag-ma-Fuff: is a dialect nickname given to a garrulous old woman.

Fairy: is a nickname given by Cockneys to big, blundering, clumsy people of both sexes.

Falstaff see *Jumbo.*

Fangie: nickname for the ship's Dentist, who is referred to as the *fang farrier.*

Fanny: is the inseparable nickname of any man named Adams: from the name of the victim of a gory murder (*c.* 1812) whose body was cut up and dumped in a river. It is very popular in the Services where 'Sweet Fanny

Adams' (or 'Sweet F.A.') is euphemistic for 'sweet f—— all', i.e. nothing. The nickname is also bestowed upon men named Fields —from 'Happy Fanny Fields' of late XIX C. music-hall fame, but the contemporary popularity of Gracie Fields, the brilliant comedienne from Lancashire, has inhibited the use of *Fanny* for a man named Fields, *Gracie* being substituted.

Fat-belly see *Jumbo.*

Fat-duck see *Jumbo.*

Father Bunloaf: an uncomplimentary term of reference, used by Irish Protestants for a Catholic priest.

Father Christmas: a nickname for, and, more commonly, a term of reference to a bearded man, particularly if he is elderly, and more particularly if he is amiable as well. (The American equivalent is *Santa*—from Santa Claus.)

Fatima see *Jumbo.*

Fats see *Fatty.*

Fatso see *Fatty.*

Fattocks see *Smallocks.*

Fatty: inevitable nickname for any fat man or boy. It invariably refers to soft, blubbery fat, not to a 'stout' figure. In modern times it is often reduced to *Fats*, and in very modern times to *Fatso*, both of which are American.

Fatty Arbuckle see *Jumbo*.

Fay: shortened form of *Ofay* [q.v.].

Filipinyock: is an American nickname for a Filipino. It may be from a combination of *Filipino* and *Yock*, which is vulgar Yiddish back-slang rendering of *goy*, which is itself a word (either Yiddish or Hebrew) used in good faith by polite Jews meaning 'a stranger' hence *Filipinyock*, a stranger of that nationality. However, *Honyock* is an American nickname for 'a farmer'.

Fire and Lights: an old Navy nickname, now obsolete, for the Master-at-Arms.

Fire-bucket see *Beetroot*.

Fire-head see *Beetroot*.

Fireworks: is a nickname given to a short-tempered person. It is a XIX C. term, as is *Pepper(pot)*, but *Bomb* appears to be recent: not before the Second War.

Fishface: is a Cockney nickname often given to a long-faced pale-complexioned man. It is inevitable if he has, into the bargain, bleary eyes.

Fishy: is an inevitable nickname given to any man whose surname is that of a fish, as Salmon, Pyke, Herring, Chubb.

Fissog: is a misspelling of *Phizog* [q.v.].

Fisty: is a North of England nickname for a person who has only one hand.

Fitsy: is a nickname given to a bad-tempered person of either sex. It has currency both here and in America. From *fits* of temper.

Five Ones: nickname for a naval Lieutenant who holds first-class certificates in each of his examinations.

Flab see *Jumbo*.

Flag (or **The Flag**): is a military term of reference to the Colour-Sergeant. Recorded by Robert Blatchford, *My Life in the Army* (1910).

Flagstaff (or **Flagpole**): is a nickname given to a weedy youth.

Flame see *Beetroot*.

Flamingo: is an American nickname for a person from Belgium—a Fleming.

Flange-face: recorded by Wentworth and Flexner, as 'a homely sailor'. Used in the U.S. Navy during the Second War.

Flange-head: nickname for a Chinaman used in the American Air Force during the Second War. Recorded by Wentworth and Flexner (1960).

Flannelmouth: is an American nickname for an Irishman.

Flap-ears: is a general nickname for an inquisitive person.

Flapper: is the inseparable nickname of any man named Hughes.

Flaps see *Lugs*.

Flarey see *Beetroot*.

Flatty: is a term of reference to a police constable. From the policeman's alleged flat feet, induced by 'pounding the beat', but also punning 'flat', a greenhorn, a fool, a dupe. [*Flat*: that with which, and in which, the ambitious girl would not live.] Children are lavish with disparaging nicknames for policemen. Iona and Peter Opie, who have miraculously broken into the Juvenile Freemasonry, give, in *The Lore and Language of Schoolchildren* (1959) p. 369: ' "We have all sorts of taunts and jeers for policemen," says a twelve-year-old in Edinburgh's Royal Mile. "We are playing at football in the street when the old flatfoot comes striding down the road. His name is P.C. Wallace but we call him old Walrus. When he has gone round the corner we call names such as Slop, Natter-Knob, Flat-feet." There are, in the London area, at least thirty nicknames current among boys, and any lad of wit [what Cockney kid is not?] seems to be able to recite a string of them. They include: Bobby [q.v.], Blueboy, Boy in Blue, Bluebottle, Blue-jacket, Blue Lamp Boy, [the average Cockney street-boy is almost certainly making an oblique reference to *Red Lamp*], Beetle, Beetle-crusher, Beatbasher, Bogey, Brass-bonce, Busy-bee, Cop, Copper [q.v.], Coppernob [q.v.], Crook-catcher, Dick, Fly, Flatfoot or Flatty, Kipperfoot, The Law [American influence in this one], Nark or Narker, Pavement-pounder, Peeler [q.v.], Robert, Rozzer or Bozzer, Slop, Snobber, and Trapper . . . Ha'penny Bogey . . . Scrufty or Scrufter. . . . In Manchester the names Penny and Shilling are sometimes used as 'comic' alternatives to Copper.'

It is also a gipsy's nickname for one who lives in a van during the summer but has a house to dwell in during the winter: a half gipsy. From *Flatty bouch*, a Romany word—half-and-half.

Flea see *Midge*.

Flight: is the nickname given to a Flight Sergeant R.A.F. Sometimes *Chiefy*.

Flinter: a Yorkshire dialect term of reference to, and a nickname for, a drunken woman.

Flip: is a nickname given to a Filipino in U.S.A. It is created by short-circuiting the word.

Flipmejig: is a Devonshire dialect nickname for a flirtatious girl.

Floan: is a Scottish and North of England dialect nickname for a lazy, untidy woman.

Floury: is an inseparable nickname for any man named Baker.

Florrie: inseparable nickname of any man named Ford. It is not derived from cheap American motor-cars, but from Florrie Ford, a popular music-hall 'turn'. This, like so many of the inseparable nicknames, had its origin in the Navy.

Fluff: is a nickname often bestowed by Cockneys on girls and young women—it is a friendly name, and generally goes to a girl who is modest and domesticated.

Fly see *Flatty*.

Fly-up-the-Creek: nickname applied to the inhabitants of Florida, U.S.A.

Fogorn (Fog horn): is a friendly nickname used by Costers, and by Racecourse 'workers' for a man with a particularly deep and loud voice.

Fogrum: is a term of reference applied in Yorkshire to one with old-fashioned ideas—a fogey.

Foolie: is a kindly and patronizing nickname used in Scotland and the North of England, when addressing one of inferior mental power.

Football see *Jumbo*.

Fortune Seekers: one of the nicknames of the inhabitants of Idaho, U.S.A.

Foureyes: a nickname which was, in the late XIX C. and early XX C., thrust upon any child of school age who was put into spectacles by the 'School doctor'. Because the name savoured of ridicule, and implied inferiority, many boys would not use the glasses—a matter very easily arranged by taking them off when in the playground and stamping on them. The spectacles supplied at that period were in rigid blue-steel frames that cut wickedly into the nose and ears, which was another, and even better, reason for destroying them. 'Four-eyed George' was the nickname of General George Gordon Mead (1815–72) of the American Army: from his wearing spectacles.

Foxes: nickname applied to the inhabitants of Maine, U.S.A.

Foxy: is the inseparable nickname of any man named Reynolds, from a similarity to Reynard.

Fraidy-cat: is a juvenile nickname for any boy or girl who displays cowardice or timidity. Sometimes it takes the form of *Scaredy-cat*.

Frank: was a nickname given to a Dutchman. Mid-XIX C., and of underworld usage. Now obsolete.

Freak: is a nickname used by children for an overgrown contemporary. Recorded by I. and P. Opie in *Lore and Language of Schoolchildren* (1959).

Freckle-faced faggot see *Zambuk*.

Freckles see *Zambuk.*

Freddy: a nickname sometimes given to a German prisoner, and also used as a general term of reference to the enemy during the 1914–18 war. From 'Friedrich'.

Frencher: is an American general nickname for a Frenchman.

Frenchy: is a nickname likely to be given to any foreigner, but particularly to a Frenchman. Popular during XIX Cent., now obsolescent.

Fresh(er): is a nickname given to a newcomer to an American university. Shortened form of 'freshman'. Sometimes altered to *Frosh.*

Fritz: nickname for a German. Popular during the 1914–18 war, but not overworked during the Second War. In the American underworld it is very aptly applied to a person subject to epileptic fits. (From Hitler's fit-like frenzy on the platform.)

Froggy: a term of reference applied to any Frenchman, and the inseparable nickname of any man with a 'French-sounding' surname. Before it was applied to Frenchmen it was applied to Dutchmen—XVII C. It also is given to a man with a wide mouth.

Froglander: is a nickname given to a Dutchman in U.S.A.

Frosh see *Fresh.*

Frowdy: a Scottish and North of England dialect nickname for a slatternly woman.

Fudge: is a nickname for a short fat person; Yorkshire and Lancashire dialect.

Fury see *Beetroot.*

Fuse-wire see *Skinnigut.*

Fusspot: is a nickname for a person who is intolerant, and ready to register complaints on slight justification. From *fuss* plus *pot*, a pot full of fuss.

Fustiluggs: 'a fulsome, beastly, nasty woman.' *The Universal Etymological Dictionary*, 3rd edn. Nathaniel Bailey, 1737.

Fuzz: is an American nickname for a policeman. Dated 1931. Recorded by D. W. Maurer, quoted by Wentworth and Flexner (1960).

G

G.I.: a nickname used during the Second War for American soldiers (by extension, also for the British girls when they married—'G.I. Brides'). Derived from 'General Issue', a U.S.A. commissariat cliché to 'brand' articles of clothing and equipment, having no special characteristic such as 'out-size', or 'left-handed'—hence, ordinary, commonplace, standard.

Gabby: is a nickname often bestowed on one who talks too much, and who is without discretion. In the underworld the name functions as a warning, in the same way as an X-shape score from a razor-slash on the face of an informer does. From Gab, the mouth.

Gaffer: is a term of address to any elderly man: it is complimentary, expressing respect for age. It is a formation, via, *Granfer*, or Grandfather—the head of the family hence, one in authority. The affectionate nickname of Sir Basil Henriques, Kt., J.P., Chairman of East London Juvenile Court, founder of Bernard Baron Settlement.

Galway: nickname for a Catholic priest used by American tramps. County Galway, Ireland, is solidly Catholic, and many Galway men emigrated to the U.S.A. in late XIX C.

Gammy: a nickname for a person who walks with a limp.

Gangy: is a XIX C. nickname for a negro. It still has some currency, and is often pronounced (hence spelt) *Kangy*.

Gannet: nickname used in the Navy for any man with a voracious appetite. The gannet is the Solan Goose (*sula bassana*).

Garbo: is a nickname given to the Dustman in Australia. From *Garbage*, but having an oblique reference to Greta Garbo.

Garron: is a term of reference, used in Ireland, in relation to a fat, slatternly woman. From *Garron*, a low-grade, bulky horse.

Gasso: is a general nickname and term of reference given by electricians to gas-fitters (and their pipes). From *gas* with suffix 'o'.

Gate: a nickname for an incessant chatterer. Although largely used in the Navy, it is probably of Cockney origin. From 'Gate' the mouth, i.e. the entrance. The term became popular during the 1914–18 war, but even by 1910 it had travelled as far as New Zealand.

Gaucho: is a nickname given by Central and Eastern European Jews to those who claim Spanish or Portuguese descent.

Gawby: is the inevitable nickname of any man from Morley. Originally Morley, Yorkshire, *gawby* being the dialect pronunciation of 'goby', a simpleton, but extended to include those from various other Morleys: Cheshire, Derbyshire, Durham and Devon (Moreleigh).

Gawm (or **Gorm**): is a nickname applied to a fool. It seems to be exclusively Cockney. There is an American word pronounced the same but variously spelt meaning sticky—gummed, but there does not seem to be a connection. Charles Dickens uses it as a mild oath—to be gormed— in this sense it is a euphemism of 'God damn', but even that sheds no light on the Cockney usage.

Geech or **Geechee**: is a nickname used in U.S.A. for a native of Georgia, or of South Carolina: but Wentworth and Flexner give it as used only for Southern negroes, and derive it from 'gullah', the Southern negro dialect.

Geechie: is a nickname given by the American Navy to girls in the Pacific Islands. The term was used also by the U.S. Army during the Second War.

General (military rank): is a nickname, used in the Southern and the Western States of U.S.A. for a tall man.

Genius see *Enos*.

Gentleman bunts: a term of reference to a signalman in the R.N.V.R.

Geordie: nickname for anyone from Newcastle, or its vicinity: employed in the Navy, but not of naval origin, being derived from Tyneside dialect: the local shape of *Georgie*.

George: a friendly term of address to any stranger, chiefly British in usage, but has some currency in both Canada and U.S.A. On the American Continent, however, and particularly in Canada, it is inclined to be narrowed down to a friendly address to a negro.

Gerty: was the nickname used during the Second War for female van drivers.

Giblets: is a jocular nickname

for either a fat person, particularly one with a protruding abdomen, or a thin person. The O.E.D. says it is a term of contempt when applied to a person; which is correct only in so far as the word is used in description: e.g. 'Caw bloimey! Swelp me if that bleet'n' great bag o' giblets ain't bin an' done it wrong agin!' This usage is, however, very rare, and it refers not to the culprit's figure, but to the fact of his being empty of anything except entrails. As a nickname it carries no inference of contempt. Sometimes shortened to *Gib*.

Giddy lamp-post: Children's nickname for a weedy boy. Recorded by I. and P. Opie in *Lore and Language of Schoolchildren* (1959) 'the idea being that he is so tall it makes one giddy'.

Gillie: is the inseparable nickname of any man named Potter: from Gillie Potter, the brilliant and amusing broadcaster of 'News from Hogsnorton'. Mr. Potter's given name was Gilbert hence, in his case, 'Gillie' was a diminutive, not a nickname. His audience covered a wide range of social strata hence, *Gillie* for any Potter, irrespective of his given name, is employed in circles where other inseparables do not penetrate. It is also a dialect nickname for a saucy, flirtatious young girl, from *Gill* (or *Jill*) *flirt*. In Scotland it is a friendly term of address between neighbours and is applied to either sex: from *gillie* or *ghillie*, the attendant upon a hunter.

Gimpy: is a general nickname bestowed upon a supremely lively or active person. It is used exclusively in the U.S.A., but is of British dialect origin.

Ginee see *Guin(ea)*.

Ginge see *Beetroot*.

Ginger: is the inseparable nickname in the Navy, and to some extent in other Services, of any man named either Jones or Smith. It is also the inseparable nickname of any man named Beer, Beers or Beare (when pronounced *beer*, from ginger-beer, the non-alcoholic drink: but when pronounced *bare*, see *Teddy*). It is, further, the general nickname for, and term of reference to, any person of either sex having auburn hair.

Ginger-conk see *Beetroot*.

Ginger-mop see *Beetroot*.

Ginger-nob see *Beetroot*.

Ginger-Tom see *Beetroot*.

Gingy see *Beetroot*.

Ginzo: is an American nickname for an Italian. Recorded by A. A. Roback, in *A Dictionary of International Slurs* (1946) but according to Wentworth and Flexner (quoting Runyon) for any foreigner.

Gippo see *Gyppo*.

Gipsy: is one of the inseparable nicknames of any man named Smith: from Gipsy Smith, the famous preacher: in addition, it is inseparable from Lee, or Leigh. It is also an admiring, and almost inevitable nickname for a girl with dark hair, eyes and complexion.

Girlie: is the inevitable nickname of the first female child born to parents who have hitherto been 'blessed' by an unbroken run of sons.

Gitty or **Gittsey:** is a term of endearment for a baby or young child in Scotland and North of England, but it becomes a nickname when it is retained after infancy has passed.

Glow-worm see *Beetroot*.

Glutton(s) see *Jumbo* and *Hungry-guts*.

Goatsuckers: a nickname applied to men of Wicklow, Ireland, particularly by men of Wexford.

Gob: is a term of reference to, and a nickname for, a U.S. sailor. Chiefly of Canadian usage.

Gobble-gobble-Gertie see *Hungry-guts*.

Gobble-guts see *Hungry-guts*.

Goddam: a nickname employed, at least till the end of the Napoleonic Wars, by Frenchmen, to Englishmen: from the Englishman's alleged habit of 'God damning' everybody and everything.

Goffer: is the nickname used in the Navy for a man or 'firm' selling mineral-waters. Frank Bowen explains that such drinks (and other little luxuries) are 'frills' on normal fare. The term developed in the first decade of XX C., as indeed the 'soft drinks industry' did.

Gold-hunters: nickname of the natives and inhabitants of California, U.S.A.

Goldilocks: nickname of, and term of reference to, any girl with golden hair, either natural or coloured artificially. It can be traced back to mid-XVI Cent. In mid-XX C. there is a tendency to reduce it to *Goldie*.

Goober: a nickname used in U.S.A. for natives of Georgia, Alabama, and of North Carolina. From *nguba*, an African word for the peanut. *Goober-grabber* may be applied to any Rustic.

Goody: is an old-fashioned nickname for a pious, domesticated girl, who stays home to help mother and hopes for a fairy-prince on horseback who will arrive at the door and marry her. She generally dies a virgin, physically, morally and mentally.

Goofy see *Enoch*.

Goo-goo: is an American Navy nickname for a Filipino, taken over by the U.S. Army during the Second War and applied to a Pacific Islander (male).

Gook: is an American term of reference applied to any dark- or swarthy-skinned person or ethnic group.

Gooly: is an inseparable nickname of any man named Ball. From the XIX C. slang word *goolies*, testicles; itself perhaps from *gully*, a word employed by street-boys to describe a number of different games that demand a gully or gutter for the scene of operations. Among such games was one of marbles.

Goon: is probably the same as *Gook* [q.v.] but may also be applied to a 'strong arm man'.

Goose (pl. **geese**): an American term of reference applied to a Jew or Jews. Recorded by Damon Runyon.

Goosey: is the inseparable nickname of any man named Gander. From the nursery rhyme:
Goosey goosey gander,
Where do you wander?

Gophers: nickname of the inhabitants of Minnesota, and of Arkansas, U.S.A. From a hard-shell land tortoise common to those States, *Gopherus polyphremus*.

Gor-belly: is a nickname given in the North of England, and in the West Country, to either a glutton, or to a pendulous-bellied person.

Gorblimey: in the category of nicknames is a descriptive term of any Londoner, applied by provincials, as a 'Bow bell' was in the reign of Elizabeth I. When not used as descriptive of a person it is generally applied to something in the way of Service dress that is rather daring —particularly to a Service cap with the wire stretcher removed, and pulled out of shape to look like a coster-monger's cloth cap. It implies a devil-may-care swagger. From 'God blind me', the prevalent Cockney expression that never means what it says.

Gordelpus: is a nickname frequently bestowed by Cockneys on people who habitually wear a sour expression, and continually complain of the hardness of their lot: 'God help us'.

Gorgey see *Hungry-guts*.

Goring: is a nickname given to a crude, brutal, troublesome man. Its use is confined to Cornwall, where Lord Goring (1608–1657) did nothing to endear himself to his neighbours.

Gosak: is an Irish nickname for a bovine, stupid person: a fool. From *Goshawk*, a falcon, *Astur palumbarius.*

Gothamite: is a nickname applied by Americans to any one from New York City. It arises from Washington Irving's story *Three Wise Men of Gotham.*

Goulash: is an American nickname for a Hungarian. From the name of the Hungarian version of Irish stew.

Goum: is an American term of reference alluding to any foreigner.

Gracie see *Fanny*.

Granite boys: nickname applied to the inhabitants of New Hampshire, U.S.A.

Gran-ma (Grandmother): is a kindly and respectful nickname used, particularly by Cockneys, in addressing any old woman. The good intention can, however, lead to the hellish retort: 'I ain't no gran-mother, young man! I ain't never bin married—so there!'

Granny: is the inseparable nickname of any man named Henderson in the Navy; and of men named Hudson in the Army. It is given by Cockneys to any mean, fussy, narrow and nagging man.

Grasshopper: a nickname for a Bluecoat girl used by the boys at Hertford School.

Gray: is an American negro's term of reference to a white man.

Grease-ball: is an American term of reference to any Southern European, or a native of the Southern American Continent.

Greaser: General nickname for a Mexican. It is of American origin, but is used in other English-speaking countries—including England—as a nickname for a man of swarthy appearance, irrespective of his nationality, but generally confined to one of Latin race.

Great Knife see *Big Knife*.

Greedy-devil see *Hungry-guts*.

Greedy-glutton see *Hungry-guts*.

Greedy-grabs see *Hungry-guts*.

Greedy-guts see *Guts.*

Greedy-hog see *Hungry-guts.*

Greedy-muffin see *Hungry-guts.*

Greedy-pig see *Hungry-guts.*

Greek: is an American nickname for an Irishman.

Green Mountain boys: nickname applied to the inhabitants of Vermont, U.S.A.

Gretchen: is a nickname for a German girl or woman in U.S.A.

Griffin: is a nickname used in U.S.A. for a Mulatto.

Grindstone (Old) see *Enos.*

Gringo: is a nickname bestowed in humour by one Englishman upon another in South America. When used by Mexicans and Amero-Spanish speakers in places south, it is the word meaning (not a nickname for) an Englishman. From *Gringo*, gibberish. Cf. the Standard Dictionary at *Barbarian.*

Grip: is the nickname given in American 'show-business' to the stage-carpenter's mate. Probably from the fact that he holds things while the master-hand saws, or screws or hammers.

Groupy: is the nickname given to a Group Captain R.A.F.

Grouser: is a general nickname for a person who is continually raising complaints. It may be rendered *grousey.*

Grouty: is a nickname for a scolding woman: peculiar to the Northern States of America.

Grubtub see *Jumbo.*

Grump(y): is a nickname given to a person who continually expresses irritation, and who will not make himself agreeable—of either sex.

Guard's van see *Muttoned.*

Gubbins: is the inevitable nickname of a native of Dartmoor.

Guin(ea): is an American nickname for an Italian. Sometimes spelt *ginee.*

Gulliver: is a nickname employed by children for an overgrown boy. Referring to Gulliver's outstanding height when in Lilliput. Recorded by I. and P. Opie, in *Lore and Language of Schoolchildren* (1959).

Gump: is a mid-XIX C. American nickname for a fool. The term had fallen into desuetude but was revitalized by the appearance of a strip-cartoon character: from a shortening and inversion of *gumption.*

Gunboat: one of the rather numerous nicknames bestowed upon a man named Smith. 'Gunboat Smith' was a pugilist of some fame who flourished early XX C.

Gunflint: is the nickname applied in U.S.A. to natives and inhabitants of Rhode Island.

Gunner: is the inseparable nickname of any man named Moor, Moore or Muir, from the famous boxer: it is also the inevitable nickname of a man

3

with one eye, from the fact of a rifleman closing one eye when sighting. In the underworld, when a one-eyed man is so nicknamed, the reference is not to a gun, but to *gonorrhoea*, which often causes blindness.

Gunnery Jack: nickname for the Gunnery Officer in H.M. ships. It is employed chiefly by ratings; fellow officers call him 'Guns'.

Guns see *Gunnery Jack*.

Guppy: a nickname used only in South Wales, applied to a person of spendthrift habits. Guppy was (is?) the name of a company having 'chain' boot and shoe shops in the Principality hence, Guppy, possessing many shops each stocked with many boots is 'well booted': an equivalent term to the more universal 'well britched', well off, wealthy, hence, 'Look you! There goes Guppy Evans in another suit indeed. He never saves a penny, man.'

Gussy: is a Cockney nickname for any young man who over-dresses and assumes airs and graces. From the name of a character in a penny weekly school-story magazine current before 1914. Used as a term of reference, it is likely to be lengthened to *Gussy-odd-socks* or — -*hot-socks*.

Guts: is the inevitable nick-name attached to a man of a notably greedy nature. In, for example, a cook-shop (or 'caff'), where he is on reasonably good terms with other habitués he is hardly likely to finish a meal without, at some point in its progress, being reminded of his notability. For example, 'Look aht pudd'n—Guts 'as got yeh!!' or the warning might have been handed to the sausages and mash! It is used in both Services, but seems to be Cockney in origin: further, it is a reduced form of 'Greedy Guts', but is very seldom used in full. 'Gutsy' is more common. It may occasionally be applied to one with a pendulous abdomen.

Guts-ache see *Hungry-guts*.

Gutsy see *Guts*.

Gutsy-sod see *Hungry-guts*.

Gutter see *Hungry-guts*.

Guy: is the inseparable nick-name of any man named Vaughan. It is also a term of reference and of address to any male person: 'That guy gets on my wick!' 'Come on, guy, drink up.' It is substitutional for 'man'. A borrowing from American English.

Guzzler see *Hungry-guts*.

Gwenny: is a nickname given to gunners in the Navy. Probably a form of *gun(ny)* influenced by Gwen(nie) short for Gwendoline, a (mainly Welsh) feminine given name.

Gyppo: is the general nick-name for the cook in the Army: from gyppo, or gippo, gravy. It is also the inevitable nickname for a native of Egypt, and in this sense is current in both the Navy and the Army.

H

Hack: is an American negro's term of reference to a white man.

Hackie: is an American nickname for a taxi-driver.

Hackney: is the inseparable nickname of any man named either Downs or Marsh. Hackney Downs and Hackney Marsh are both items of London topography, hence the term must be of Cockney origin, but in the Services it is used by men from the provinces.

Haggis: is a disparaging nickname given by Cockneys to a particularly 'dour' Scot. From the name of the famous Scottish dish.

Hair-bones see *Skinnigut*.

Hair-cut: is a nickname given by Cockneys to any man who habitually wears his hair ostentatiously long.

Hairpin see *Skinnigut*.

Hake: general nickname for any man who is a native of St. Ives. Imported into the Navy by Cornishmen, and down to the end of the XIX C., resented by those who received it.

Half-pint see *Midge*.

Half Ringer see *Ringer*.

Hammy-bones see *Jumbo*.

Handkerchief-head: is an American nickname for a submissive, meek negro, who retains the house-boy slave mentality.

Handsome: is, by the humour of inversion, a general nickname for anyone with rugged features: 'handsome in an ugly kind of way'. In London, it is, in addition, a term of affectionate address to a bull-dog, or bull-terrier.

Hannah: nickname for a Wren afloat, serving with the Marines: from Hannah Snell, who, masquerading as a man, served at sea in the XVIII C., and whose sex was not discovered—even when she was wounded—till the end of her service.

Hans: is a general nickname for a German. It has a greater currency in the U.S.A. than in England.

Ha'penny Bogey see *Flatty*.

Happy see *'appy*.

Hardcases: nickname of the inhabitants of Oregon, U.S.A.

Hard-head: is a two-way American term of reference. Applied by white men to negroes it means physically hard—and empty. Applied by negroes to white men it means crude, lacking in finer feeling and understanding.

Harman: is a nickname applied to a policeman by the American underworld. It is of British origin.

Harp(y): is a nickname for an Irishman in U.S.A.

Harry: is the inseparable nickname of any man named Freeman: from the expression 'It's Harry Freemans' to describe anything for which no payment is made: as 'He smokes Harry Freemans [cigarettes] never buys his own!' or 'You can get into The Bugodrome Harry Freemans, if you're in uniform, before 4 o'clock.'

Hatchet: a naval nickname for any man who habitually wears a 'long face'; also, any man who is hollow-cheeked. It is a shortening of *hatchet-faced*.

Hatchet-thrower: is an American term of reference to a Cuban. Probably from a reputation for skill and accuracy in knife-throwing.

Havercake: is a nickname sometimes given to one from Lancashire.

Hawkeye: a general nickname used in U.S.A. for anyone from Iowa.

Hawkins (pronounce *'Awkins*): is a Cockney term of reference to an exacting employer. It is now obsolescent since the most exacting of employers fears the Union-supported revolt of all employees in support of the least exact of them. Said to be derived from Judge (hanging) Hawkins.

Hay-eater: is an American negro's nickname for a white man.

He-Face: Eric Partridge says 'A Public Schools' esp. Harrovian nickname for men surnamed Baker. Ex. *he*, a cake', (see *A Covey* of Partridge).

Hedgehog: a London Bluecoat School boy's nickname for a boy from the Hertford School. Those from Hertford retorted with *Jackdaws*, now obsolete.

Heebie: is an American nickname for a Jew. From *Hebrew*. Recorded by Damon Runyon, who spells it *Heeb*.

Heinie: nickname for a German. It was used largely in the 1914–18 war, and since then has become general.

Hellfire Jack: old sailing dogs' nickname for an intrepid officer.

Herkimer Jerkimer: is an American nonsense name applied to anyone whose name is unknown, but particularly to a rustic, or to a simpleton.

Herring Choker (sometimes pronounced 'Joker'): is an American nickname for an inhabitant of New Brunswick: also for a Scandinavian.

Hick: a term of reference applied to a countryman, by American town-dwellers. See also *Rube*.

Hinkty: an American negro's

term of reference to a white man.

Hitler (also 'Mrs. Hitler'): is a defiant nickname literally hurled at all domineering, interfering and aggressive people.

Hodge: a once popular nickname for a farm-hand, but in these days of television and motor cycles Hodge is as up-to-date as any townee. The vendors of genuine diamond rings, sold at a sacrifice to advertise their firm's goods, find more buyers on Charing Cross Road than at Little Muddicombe Fair. ['Hodge' was the name, not the nickname, of Dr. Johnson's cat.]

Hog: is a nickname for a native of Hampshire. It can be traced as far back as the XVII C. From the superior breed of pigs produced in that county. See also *Hungry gut*.

Hogan Mogan: is an American nickname given to Dutchmen. From *hoog mogenheden*, i.e. 'high mightiness'.

Hollow-legs see *Hungry-guts*.

Holy Joe: is a Cockney term of reference to a person who is ostentatiously pious.

Hombre: is a term of address used in U.S.A. It is now, particularly in the Northern States, jocular: but in the South West it is taken seriously and applied only to one of Spanish ancestry.

Honyock see *Filipinyock*.

Hooky: is one of the inseparable nicknames of any man

named Walker. From the retort 'Walker!' mid-XIX C. equivalent to the modern 'I *don't* think!' meaning it is not true, or it will not take place. John Bee, in his *Dictionary*, 1823, gives the origin as derived from one John Walker, a hook-nosed spy and champion liar. (See *Johnny*.) The Navy has a different version: John Walker, they say, was the outdoor clerk of Messrs. Longman Clementini & Co., late of Cheapside, and was noted for his large hooked nose. He is supposed to have flourished in the 1880's. Further naval usage is as a nickname for a leading seaman, from the anchor badge by which he is distinguished.

Hoosier: a general nickname used in U.S.A. for anyone from Indiana.

Hopkins (sometimes preceded by Mr.): nickname for a person who walks with a limp.

Hopper: is one of the inseparable nicknames of a man named Long.

Hoppy: the nickname of anyone who walks with a limp. Although such a reference to a deformity may seem cruel to persons not accustomed to the ways of Cockneys, it should be understood that no cruelty is intended, nor is the nickname resented by those who receive it—in fact, on the principle of 'there is only one thing worse than being talked about, and that is not being talked about', failure to give the name might be regarded as offensive.

Horace see *'Orris.*

Horner, Miss: is a term of reference applied to a girl with a hospitable thigh.

Horse, Old: is a nickname applied to anyone, either because his name is unknown, or because one wishes to express conviviality as: 'I say, Jock, what'll yeh have, old horse?' Sometimes *Old top* is used.

Hot and Cold: is the inseparable nickname of any man whose initials are H.C., from the hot and cold water taps over both basin and sink, emphasized in Estate Agents' advertisements.

Hotbot, Miss (or **Lady**)**:** is a nickname applied to any girl often seen in the company of men.

Howty: is a nickname given to a bad-tempered person. Scottish dialect.

Huge-Paw: an American nickname for a rough, uncouth person. Originally a term of disparagement for a farmer, later for backwoodsmen, finally for a left-wing power-politics faction in New York. Now obsolescent.

Human-tank see *Jumbo.*

Hungry-guts: a nickname invariably applied to a person who is constantly eating. (Such a one, among Cockneys, is said to be suffering from the *metasses*—a word which seems to have been shaped out of some similar sounding Yiddish word.) Children appear to be particularly critical: Iona and Peter Opie, in *The Lore and Language of Schoolchildren* (1959) p. 176, have the following: 'They call him [the greedy boy] dustbin [q.v.], hollow-legs, hog, face-packer, gluttons, gobble-guts, Gobblegobble-Gertie, Gorgey, greedyglutton, greedy-devil, greedygrabs, greedy-hog, greedymuffin, greedy-pig . . . guts [q.v.] guts-ache, gutsy-sod, gutter, guzzler, guzzle-guts, hungry-guts [q.v.], hungry-Horace, piggy, pig-hog, piganog (pig- an'-'og), pig-bin, rumble tummy.'

In an accompanying note, 'The term greedy-guts is more than 400 years old. . . . The name Gobble-gobble-Gertie, on the other hand, dates only from 1954 when a perpetually ravenous Eskimo woman was featured in a *Beano* [coloured comic] picture story.'

Hungry-Horace see *Hungryguts.*

Hunky: is an American nickname for a person from Hungary.

I

I-say: now obsolete, but in the latter half of the XIX C. the general nickname used by Frenchmen for Englishmen.

Ian (pronounce *eye-an*): is the inseparable nickname of a man named Low, or Lowe: punning 'High and . . .'

Idleback see *Muttoned*.

Ikey: is the inseparable nickname of any man having an Old Testament surname, and many West Country families have. It is also used as a term of address to a Jew, but less frequently than *Abie* [q.v.]. As a term of reference it is applied to a mean person.

Ikey Mo: a non-personal term of reference to a Jew, based on the common personal names *Isaac* and *Moses*.

Imp: is a friendly and affectionate nickname used largely in London, for a lively child or young person. It is also applied in the same way to domestic animals. The O.E.D. gives, *inter alia*: '5. A mischievous child (having a little of "the devil" in him); a young urchin: often used playfully.'

Ink or **Inkface:** is a nickname used for a negro in U.S.A.

Irisher: an American nickname for a person of Irish origin.

Iron: is the inseparable nickname of any man named Duke, Dukes, Juke or Jukes. From the sobriquet of Arthur Wellesley, Duke of Wellington. Sloven pronunciation suggests *Eye on* to the dim of wits, and though they are few and far between when as bad as that, they are to be met with.

Ironfoot: is the inevitable nickname of anyone who, having a withered, or otherwise shortened leg, is provided with a steel extension. The name is becoming less common as orthopaedic science provides better forms of extension and greater concealment of the defect; but many old-established 'Ironfoots' will not relinquish the steel frame: some of them trade upon it for begging, or for 'working the markets' (strangely enough, the calling of quack-doctors seems to be favoured by them). The nickname is often prefixed to a given name: 'Ironfoot Dick', 'Ironfoot 'Arry'.

'Isnibs (His nibs): is a disparaging term of reference used by Cockneys when a person 'puts on the quiver', the gentleman; or magnifies a minor amount of authority. *Nib*, and *nibs* is a form of 'nob'.

Israel: is a general nickname for a village idiot in Suffolk. It is also a descriptive term: 'If he did that he's an Israel'.

Itchlander: is an uncomplimentary term of reference applied to Scotsmen.

Itchy (or **Itchycoo**): a U.S.A. term of reference to, and nickname for, a person from Yugoslavia. According to an informant, from an old ragtime song, *Itchycoo*, and repeating the word in the chorus, but Wentworth and Flexner give '. . . from the "——ich" ending of many surnames.' Probably also influenced by *itchy*, 'lousy'.

Izzy see *Abie*.

J

Jack: is the inseparable nickname of any man named Shepherd: from the spectacular jailbreaker, Jack Shepherd, hero of Ainsworth's very readable novel of that name. It is also a friendly term of address used by Cockneys when the stranger to whom one is speaking is judged to be of a social status about equivalent to one's own. Its bestowal upon London Italians, particularly icecream vendors, had they but known it, was in the nature of a high Cockney compliment. In this usage it was current from the age of Garibaldi to that of Mussolini. It is now restored to currency and is extended to café keepers because ice-cream has got into 'big business'. Last (but not least) it is an old-established term of address to any sailor (used by lubbers more than seamen): from Jack Tar, a general reference to a sailor, evolved in XVIII C.

Jack Dusty: nickname for a supplies rating in the Royal Navy. The ship's stores is a dusty place.

Jack Nasty Face see *Nasty Face*.

Jack Shalloo: nickname for an officer who puts himself out to be popular with the ratings: from John Chellew, who was known as 'Popularity Jack'.

Jack Strop's old woman see *Stroppy*.

Jackdaw: Nickname for a London Bluecoat School boy, used particularly by boys of the Hertford School, in return for *Hedgehogs* [q.v.]. Now obsolete.

Jacker: nickname for all Cornishmen in the Navy: from *Jago* [q.v.] which is a common Cornish surname. It is also spelt Jagger.

Jacko: is a general Cockney nickname for an Italian of the street-trading class. Now obsolescent. During the 1914–18 war it was Gallipoli Forces slang, an alternative form of *Johnnie* [q.v.] for the Turks as a nation, and for an individual Turkish prisoner.

Jackoleg: is a Cockney (ex-Navy?) nickname for a tall, slender man. It is of XVIII C. origin, and is given by Grose, 1st edn. Sometimes spelt *Jackyleg*. It may be from *Jockteleg*, a long-bladed clasp-knife, itself said to be (but unproven) from 'Jacques de Liege', a famous cutler.

Jacky: general nickname for an aborigine (male) Australian: also a nickname for Admiral Sir John Fisher, who is famous for (*inter alia*) walking out of the Admiralty Board Room when the rest of the Lords of Admiralty did not agree with him.

Jacky Raw: was a general nickname for a newcomer to Australia. It was in use during the last quarter of the XIX and first quarter of XX C.

Jacky Rue: is a nickname given in Australia to a squatter.

Jacquerie: is the usual nickname given to a French girl in U.S.A.

Jagger see *Jacker*.

Jago: nickname for the Victualling Paymaster, Devonport Division: from the common Cornish surname, Jago. 'Jago's' is also the name of the mess in Devonport Naval Barracks.

Jaisy: is a nickname given to an effeminate man in the Midlands, North of England, and in Scotland. It is a dialect form of Daisy, which is equivalent in application to South of England Pansy.

Jan: is a general nickname likely to be given to a Cornishman (sometimes, 'Jackey'): but either, as a term of reference, is likely to be preceded by 'Cousin'. Largely of Canadian currency, particularly among miners.

Jap: is an American, probably Western, nickname for a professional gambler.

Jar-head: is an old Southern American nickname for a negro. During the Second War it was applied by Americans to their highly esteemed Marines.

Jarvie: is the nickname used in Ireland for the driver of a jaunting-car (equivalent of a cab). It was also the nickname used throughout the Fleet, for Admiral John Jarvis, Baron of Heaford, Earl of St. Vincent.

Jasper: is a general nickname given to a Brighton fisherman.

Jaunty: of (hardly to), the Master-at-Arms. It originated during the Napoleonic Wars when French prisoners referred to the Master-at-Arms as 'Le Gendarme' which, taken over by the Navy, became at first 'Johndy Damn', which was truncated to 'Johndy', then shaped to 'Johnty' which rounded off to 'Jaunty'.

Jawkins: nickname applied to a bore. Popular XIX C., but now obsolete, from Thackeray's *Book of Snobs*.

Jay hawkers: nickname of the inhabitants of Kansas, U.S.A.

Jaybee: is a nickname given to a negro in U.S.A. From 'J.B.', the initial letters of 'jet-black'.

Jazzboo: is a nickname used in U.S.A. for a negro.

Jeames: a general nickname for a footman. Now obsolete: a supposedly 'upper-class' pronunciation of *James*.

Jean: a nickname used at sea for any Frenchman.

Jebbel: inseparable nickname in the Army from *c.* 1920 for any man named Hill: from the Arabic word for a hill.

Jelly: is the inseparable nickname of any one named Pearson. This is believed to have originated at King Edward's School, Birmingham.

Jellywobble see *Jumbo*.

Jenny: is a nickname for, and a reference term alluding to, any member of the Wrens. (Women's Royal Naval Service.) Jenny Wren, the bird, *Troglodites Parvulus*, may be from *Jenty*. Northern dialect.

Jenny Darby: an early- to mid-XIX C. nickname for a Police Constable. From *gens d'armes*.

Jerkanese: is an American nickname for a Japanese. From *Jerk*, a person of no account.

Jerry: is the inseparable nickname of any man named either Dawson or Ring. It is, too, the general nickname of any German, and a form of address to any German prisoner.

Jesse James: is an American road-transport driver's nickname for a police magistrate. It is also applied to the umpire by baseball players.

Jesso: is the inseparable nickname of any man named Reid (Reed—Read). It is itself a form of *Jessy*, and having been in use in the Navy for at least fifty, perhaps even sixty or seventy years, its association is untraceable. Jessie Reid may have been a beer-vending matron, or even a sportive maiden, well known to the Navy in Portsmouth, Plymouth or Chatham—even Malta.

Jessy see *Jesso*.

Jewy: is the inseparable nickname of any man named Moss: from the fact that many Jews, originally surnamed *Moses*, have become 'Moss' either by deliberate change of name, or through the process of sloven pronunciation. All men named Moss are, however, not Jews.

Jibagoo: is a 'humorous' inversion of *Jigaboo* [q.v.].

Jibby: is a nickname, given in Suffolk, to an affected, dress-conscious, pleasure-seeking woman: from 'jibby-horse'—one especially groomed and decked out for a show.

Jigaboo: is an American nickname for a negro. Sometimes shortened to *Jiga* or *Jig*.

Jiggamy: is a nickname for a person whose own name is

unknown. (Also applied to objects.)

Jigger: is an alternative to *Bodger* [q.v.] the inseparable nickname of men named Lees.

Jiltar: is a rare alternative for *Jenny Wren* [q.v.].

Jim Crow: a nickname, now obsolescent, for a coloured man: from a song performed by Thomas D. Rice, the first negro minstrel, Washington, 1835.

Jimmo: is the Cockney pronunciation of Dimmo, from Demo, short for Demosthenes, a common given name, hence nickname, for any Greek, but particularly a café keeper.

Jimmy: is the inseparable nickname of any man named Riddell: from Jimmy Riddle, rhyming slang on *piddle*, to urinate. It is also an inseparable nickname for any man named Green. In Australia it is a general term of address to a 'new chum'—an 'Immy' (short for Immigrant).

Jimmy Bungs: was the name bestowed upon the cooper in the days when barrels, casks and tubs were an essential part of a ship's fittings and equipment. Today, fixture-tanks and steel drums are used, and the ships do not need a cooper.

Jimmy Ducks: nickname for the ship's poulterer.

Jimmy Grant: *emigrant* (particularly one going to Australia), XIX C., now obsolete.

Jimmy the One: of (not to) the First Lieutenant in the Navy.

Jimmy Rounds: nickname bestowed by the Navy upon Frenchmen in Nelson's time— from their cry of *je me rends*.

Jingler see *Enos*.

Jit: is an American nickname for a negro, from jitney, a five-cent piece hence, a thing of small value.

Jock: nickname for any Scotsman used in all Services and universally by civilians. 'He's a Jock', means he is a Scot: 'Here come the Jocks' signals the approach of a Highland regiment—for whom the Germans were never known to wait.

Joe: is the inseparable nickname of any man named Beckett, from the boxer, hence *c.* 1919: it is also a general nickname for anyone whose own name is unknown; and, in America, the general nickname for a Filipino.

Joe Bag(gs): is an American hotel servants' nickname for a guest who does not give tips— the inference is, apparently, that he is a commercial traveller. In some houses *Joe M'Gee* is used.

Joe Blow: is a nickname given to a performer on a wind-instrument. American musicians.

Joe Bunker: a now obsolete general nickname for an American citizen, used by Americans.

Joe Doakes (sometimes *Joe Doe*): is an American general term of reference to the average man: any member of the American proletariat. Sometimes rendered *John Doe*.

Joe Doe see *Joe Doakes*.

Joe M'Gee see *Joe Bag(gs)*.

Joey: name bestowed upon any clown who wears the traditional uniform, and carries through the classical act: from Joseph Grimaldi.

Joey Major: nickname for a Major of the Royal Marines.

John: is a nickname used in America for any Chinaman. Short form of *John* or *Johnny Chinaman*.

John Blunt see *Blunther*.

John Bull: a universal nickname for the English nation, or for a 'typical' Englishman. The popularity of the term has been steadily waning since *c.* 1918.

John Doe see *Joe Doakes*.

John Plush: nickname for a footman: from his plush breeches. Now as obsolete as the servant himself. Originated by Thackeray in *The Yellowplush Papers* (1837).

John Q. Citizen (or **John Q. Public**): is an American term of reference to the average man: it is interchangeable with *Joe Doakes* [q.v.].

Johndal: is a nickname given to the junior ploughman on a Scottish farm.

Johnny: is one of the inseparable nicknames of a man named Walker. It is derived from the name of the famous brand of whisky whose advertising phrase '1820 not out' became an early XX C. catchphrase. In addition, it is the inseparable nickname, in the Navy, for any man named Bone. Wilfred Granville says (letter dated 2 March 1960), '*Johnny Bone* was a great smuggler ashore of unconsidered trifles (a *rabbiter*, or scrounger). He was Boatswain to Admiral Cornwallis who remarked to him, 'I trust, Mr. Bone, that you will leave me my anchor.' Hence, maybe, the verb *to bone*?" It is also a term of address to any Turkish prisoner, and extended to *Johnny Turk*, descriptive of the entire Turkish Nation. The term, which is still employed, does not seem to ante-date the 1914–18 war when Johnny Turk earned the reputation among the troops of being 'a gentleman': that is, a clean, fair fighter. No German ever earned that high praise. It is also the nickname for a Greek.

Johnny Cake: is, in England, a dialect term of reference to a simpleton: in the U.S.A., however, it is a nickname for a native of New England.

Johnny Cheats: is a nickname used in several counties for a pedlar.

Johnny-come-fortnight: is a dialect nickname for a 'collector' working for a credit stores, or for an itinerant salesman working on his own account: for the London version see next entry.

Johnny Fortnight: was the nickname given by Cockneys to the 'tallyman', the door-to-door collector of minor hire-purchase payments prior to 1914, when such transactions were for the working-class only. (It was considered not quite decent to buy what one could not pay for at once.)

Johnny Gallagher: is a general nickname for a policeman: used chiefly by tramps. From the fact that at one time many Irishmen joined the police force.

Johnny-knock-softly: is a nickname given to leisurely workmen. Current in South of England.

Johnny Newcome: nickname used in the Merchant Navy for a new hand.

Johnny Raw: is a nickname given in the South of England to an inexperienced person, or, by townsfolk, to a rustic. *Johnny Wopstraw*, which is another version, is often applied.

Johnny Wopstraw see *Johnny Raw*.

Jollacks: is a term of reference to a clergyman. Usage seems to be confined to Suffolk.

Jonah: is the inseparable nickname of any man named Jones—from the similarity of sound.

Jonathan: is a shortened form of *Brother Jonathan* [q.v.].

Jonty: alternative form of *Jaunty* [q.v.].

Joseph: nickname for an absent-minded person—because Joseph was a dreamer.

Josh: is an American nickname for a native of Arkansas.

Josie: is the inseparable nickname of any man named Brooker. Originally naval in usage it spread to the Army and was current towards the end of the XIX C.: from Joseph Brooker, Governor of Malta, called by the natives Josie Brooker. It is also the nickname for any native of Malta serving in the Royal Navy.

Jot: is a nickname given to a short, thick-set man in Norfolk, and Suffolk. From dialect *jot*, the posterior: anything large and heavy.

Judas: is a nickname given, in some coastal areas, to a man with auburn hair. From the reputed colouring of Judas Iscariot.

Judge: is a general nickname used in the South and West of America for a fat man.

Judy: nickname used in the Navy for a policewoman. In the Army it is employed as a general term for women, and among soldiers who have served in the East it is a nickname for a Jew. From *Yehudi* (Arabic).

Juice: is the nickname given to the stage-electrician. American 'show-business'.

Jug: is a general nickname

given to any native of Brighton.

Jukey: is an American nickname applied to a tall, round-shouldered man. Perhaps from the negro word *Juke*, coitus.

Jumbo: is a nickname likely to be bestowed upon a fat man, boy, or girl, but not (as a rule) to a mature woman. It is from the name of an elephant who was a great favourite with Cockneys. When the animal was sold to Barnum, the American showman, in 1882, there was a furious outcry.

Iona and Peter Opie, in *The Lore and Language of Schoolchildren* (1959) p. 168, under the sub-title *Fatties*, give: 'Back end of a bus, balloon, barrage-balloon, barrel, barrel-belly, barrow-guts, big-belly-bump, Billy Bunter the second, blood-tub, bouncer, Buster, Chubby, Chunky, Crystal Jelly-bottom, diddle-diddle-dumpling, Falstaff, fat belly, fat duck, Fatty Harbuckle [and on whom a footnote], flab, football, glutton, grub-tub, guts [q.v.], hammy-bones, jellybelly, jelly-wobble . . . lumpy, lump-of-lardy, piggy, pillar-box, podge, porker, Porky, porridge, pud, plum-pudding, pudding-pie, rubber-guts, sausage, slob, slug, steam-roller, swell-hide, tank, human-tank, ten-ton, tubs, tubby [q.v.] (Tubus and Magnus Tubus in Grammar Schools), and Two-Ton Tessie.

'The names Bessie Bunter, Fatima, and Tubbelina, are usually reserved for girls.'

The footnote on 'Fatty Harbuckle' records that it was collected so spelt from London, Portsmouth, Oundle, Worcester; as 'Fatty Harbottle' from Birmingham, 'Fatty Arbicle' from Welshpool; and as 'Fatty Artabuckles' from Frostburg, Maryland, U.S.A. The note continues: 'None of the children who used the term, nor their teachers, realized that they were perpetuating the name of the talented corpulent comedian, Roscoe Arbuckle (1887–1933). . . .'

Jumper: the inseparable nickname of any man named Cross. A particularly witty formation unless one is of the turn of mind that denounces the best of puns as 'the lowest form of wit', and so crude a one as 'jump across' as lower still. *Jumper* is also one of the nicknames coupled to Collins; also a nickname used by London Transport workers for a ticket inspector: he jumps on unexpectedly.

Junior: is a nickname bestowed, in America, upon a male child, especially if he is the only one. It has a small currency in that sense in Britain, but its chief usage here is in the form of a mild rebuke, as 'Nah den Junior —I don't want none o' your lip.'

K

Kaintuck: is an American nickname for a native or an inhabitant of Kentucky.

Kale: is a nickname for a tall thin person. Used in Ireland, Scotland and the North of England.

Kanack see *Canuck*.

Kangy see *Gangy*.

Kelt: is an American negro's nickname for a white man.

Ketin: is the inseparable nickname used in the Army, from *c.* 1920, for any man named Braines, Brayne, Biggs, Long: from the Arabic word for 'big'.

Kettle: is a nickname given to a man named Bob (Robert). It is truncated rhyming slang, *Kettle on the hob*, a 'bob', (a shilling), but is extended to cover the given name Bob.

Kibitz: is an American nickname for one who habitually stands and watches others engaged at various occupations, and gives gratuitous advice. It comes through Yiddish from German *Kiebitz*, a spectator during card games.

Kicky or **Kicksy:** is a nickname used in Pennsylvania for, says Henry W. Shoemaker, in *Thirteen Hundred Old Time Words*, (1930), 'a hard to please, petulant, cross girl.'

Kid: is used as a nickname for any person who is noticeably young in a community of older men. It gained a wide popularity in the Army during the 1914–18 war when men of very mixed ages were serving together in the same unit. It may also become a personal nickname for anyone who achieves some sort of fame at an early age, as for example, Kid Lewis, the boxer. Such a nickname has the gift of eternal youth while its owner perceptibly ages: bestowed at the age of (say) sixteen, it will still be in use when sixty is reached.

Kiddo: is an extended form of Kid. It may be employed as a nickname for a boy, or a young man; but its general usage is as a term of address to a girl or young woman. It is not as modern as it seems, having emerged in late XIX C.

Kike: an uncommon nickname for a Jew: possibly from Ike, diminutive of Isaac, a popular Jewish masculine given name.

Killick: a term of address to a Leading Seaman. It is also descriptive of the rank. In the former function it is equivalent to 'Corp' [q.v.] for Corporal, as used in the Army. Killick is an early XVII C. word meaning anchor, and an anchor is the arm-badge of a Leading Seaman.

Kiltie: a derisive term of

address to a Highland soldier, used only when on mischief bent since the Scots resent its use, and are likely to reply with blows: (even belts).

King Bomba: nickname of Ferdinand II, King of the Two Sicilies (1810–59). He was so named from his bombardment of Messina. [This entry, which is admittedly rather out of the scope of the present work, is included solely because a very well-known firm supplying Continental provisions, in Soho, London, uses the title as a business name, and few people among the many who are familiar with the shop, know the origin of the title.]

Kinken: is an American nickname for a Circus performer: for *kink*, to bend, hence an acrobat.

Kinky-nob: is a nickname given to a negro in U.S.A., from the 'peppercorn' hair of the Negro race.

Kipper: a nickname of naval origin for any stoker, now obsolescent due to the fairly general adoption of oil-fuelled boilers; the inference being that the stoker, like the kipper, is smoked. See also *Midge*.

Kipperfoot see *Flatty*.

Kitten: is the inevitable nickname of the younger of two brothers at King Edward's School, Birmingham.

Kitty: the inseparable nickname, particularly in the Navy, of any man named either Wells, or Wills.

Kiwi: is a nickname applied to any native of or inhabitant of New Zealand: from the Kiwi, the native wingless bird. Not to be confused with *Kwewe* [q.v.].

Knickerbocker: a general nickname used in U.S.A. for anyone from New York State.

Knobby: is the inseparable nickname of any man named Coles: from *Knob*, a lump (of coal). It is a transposition from *nobby* [q.v.], and being homophonic is often spelt wrongly when used by writers of fiction.

Knocker: a nickname frequently bestowed upon naval ratings named either White or Walker. Also, as a short form of 'Knocker-face' it is a general nickname for an ugly man, or one with a habitually grim and hard expression: from a supposed likeness to a street-door knocker.

Knocky see *Nocky*.

Knowall: a nickname given (particularly by Cockneys) to any person who volunteers an explanation of everything, and who hands out unsolicited advice, and unheeded words of wisdom. Pre-1914, and possibly much older. Sometimes rendered *Know-itall*.

Kwewe see *Queue*.

Kye: is a temporary nickname used in the Navy for the rating who, during the Middle Watch (midnight to 4 a.m.) is 'told off' to make the cocoa. In the Navy, cocoa and chocolate is *Kye*.

L

L.S.D. see *Skinnigut*.

Lackery: one of the inevitable nicknames to which any man in the Navy named Wood must answer. It is from the Hindustani word *Lakri*, meaning wood.

Lady Macbeth: is an American radio producer's nickname for an actress of the super-emotional type.

Lady Marm: is a nickname favoured by Cockneys, for any girl or woman of their own social stratum who 'puts on the quiver', i.e. pretends to superiority; or for any social-worker, or woman in authority, as for example, a Labour Exchange clerk, who is, or appears to be, 'uppish', i.e. haughty in manner. *Marm* from 'madam', via '*ma'am*'.

Lagger: is a nickname given by schoolboys in London for one of their number who is a tale-bearer. To *lag* is to tell. Cockney dialect.

Lal (or **Lally**): is the usual name applied by Cockneys to any girl named Alice, but whether it is truly a nickname, or more in the nature of a diminutive, it would be hard to say.

Lally: a general nickname for an old woman, but particu-larly a tough one; or one who had enjoyed such a reputation in youth and middle age. It is seldom heard now, but was popular in late XIX C. and the first decade of XX C. It is from *Lal Brough*, rhyming slang for snuff. Many old women are snuff-takers.

Lamp-post: a Cockney nickname for any exceedingly tall person. It was more popular in the first decade of this century, when the average lamp-post was (say) ten feet high, than it now is when street lighting has been lifted skyward, out of daily life. See also *Skinnigut*.

Lamps: nicknames of the hand in charge of the ship's lamps—Merchant Navy: often rendered *Lampy*. He may be referred to as the *bati-wallah*: from Hindustani, but *bati* is not a term of address—it could lead to misunderstandings.

Langtry, Mrs. or **Lily**: was a nickname given, during the last two decades of the XIX and the first two of the XX C's, to any beautiful woman—particularly one with fine eyes. The term was used mostly by English society domiciled in Egypt. Lily Langtry (1852–1929) went on the stage in 1881 and was a phenomenal success.

Lanky: is a Standard English word for tall and thin, and is employed not merely as a term of reference to, but as a nickname for a person of that stature. It is also applied to anyone from Lancashire.

Lanky Liz see *Skinnigut*.

Lanky Panky see *Skinnigut*.

Lardy see *Muttoned*.

Law, The see *Flatty*.

Lazy: is a jocular nickname for a waitress who is notably quick, efficient and industrious. Humour by inversion, though not exclusively Cockney, is much practised by them.

Lazybird see *Muttoned*.

Lazybones see *Muttoned*.

Leather: is a nickname given in the underworld, to a pick-pocket who specializes in pocket wallets. As a term of reference it takes the form *Leather Merchant*, as, 'He is a leather-merchant', but 'Hullo, Leather, how's tricks?'

Leather-heads: one of the nicknames used in U.S.A. to refer to natives of Pennsylvania.

Lecco: is a general nickname and term of address, given by gas-fitters to electricians (and to electrical wiring conduits). From *electric*: 'lec', rounded off with 'o', which is a common suffix in many slang words, and is much favoured by Cockneys and Irishmen. Cf. *Gasso*.

Ledger bo'sun: nickname for a ship's book-keeper.

Lefty: is the inevitable nickname of any left-handed person. In *Murder at Lancaster Gate*, by F. D. Grierson, a character named Lefty Harris appears so named 'on account of his being left-handed'. It is also very often given to a man named Wright, punning, Right.

Lemon: is an American term of reference to a light-skinned negress.

Leopard see *Zambuk*.

Leslie: a nickname bestowed upon a lesbian. Australian. Recorded by Sidney J. Baker in *The Drum* (1959).

Lightning: a particularly Cockney nickname for anyone who is slow in either or both mental and physical reaction. It is as likely to be applied to a female as to a male: for example, to a waitress in a 'caff' (not to be confused with a café): 'Oi, Lightnin', git us two zepps in a clahrd—an' I wan' it fer me dinner—not fer me tea.'

Lilywhite: in America, a jocular nickname for either a negro or a chimney-sweep. In Britain, for the latter only, but now obsolescent.

Limberg: is a nickname given to any German. It has reference to Limburger, the malodorous cheese; and in the U.S.A. is so pronounced—final 'er'.

Limejuicer: an obsolete alternative for *Limey* [q.v.].

Limey: an American and Canadian nickname for an Englishman: from the lime-juice, supplied as an anti-scorbutic to British sailors. Captain James Cook is the real discoverer of vitamins. He carried sauerkraut which he induced his crew to eat by representing it as a pickle for officers only, and thus prevented scurvy. The term was, in XIX C., used in Australia for a 'new chum', but was abandoned in favour of *Pommy* [q.v.] early in XX C.

Limpsey: is a nickname given to a lazy, slothful person. From *limp*, soft, lacking firmness. Dialect.

Linkum: is a nickname given in the North of England to a pampered, spoiled person. The word is allied to *nincompoop*.

Lippy: is a Cockney nickname for a super-talkative person, particularly if he is also habitually impudent. In use before 1914. From *lip*, impudence.

Little Squirt see *Midge*.

Litvac: is an American nickname for one of Lithuanian origin. Wentworth and Flexner state that it is used jocularly.

Liza: a now obsolete American nickname for any coloured girl.

Lizards: nickname applied to inhabitants of Alabama, U.S.A.

Lob: is a nickname given to a loutish person, in the North of England. It is, and is meant to be, uncomplimentary: a gamekeeper, for example, may be so addressed. It sometimes takes the form *Lob-cock*.

Lobbus see *Lummox*.

Loblolly boy: nickname used in the Merchant Navy for a steward. Loblolly is porridge hence, the ship's cook may be called the *lolly-banger*.

Locofoco: a political nickname current in mid-XIX C. in America for a Democrat. It was originally a trade name for matches, but was applied to the Party when, having pre-knowledge that the opposition intended to turn off the gas at the main to disorganize an indoor meeting, each supporter came provided with matches and candles.

Lofty: nickname for a tall man. Of naval origin, its use has spread to other Services and into civilian life. Via the mechanism of humour by inversion it is very frequently bestowed upon a particularly small man.

Loggy: is an American and Canadian nickname for a slothful person: from *log* of wood. Originally South of England dialect.

Lolly-banger see *Loblolly-boy*.

London Closet Cleaners: a Cockney disparaging nickname for the London County Council, in use till *c.* 1910, now dead and buried too deep for there to be fears of a resurrection, for in half a century this admirable Civic Body has accomplished so much, and with such distinction, that even those Londoners who do not share its political views acknowledge, with respect, its functional achievement. This entry, admittedly beyond the scope of the work, is included on account of there being a political threat hanging over us: the L.C.C. is to be swallowed (if not digested) by a bigger, more ungainly and necessarily less efficient body provisionally styled 'Greater London Council'.

Long and Lanky see *Skinnigut*.

Long-John: is a nickname used by London schoolboys for an overgrown, weedy contemporary. From Long John Silver (*Treasure Island*), hence used by the older rather than the younger boys.

Long Knife see *Big Knife*.

Long Meg: 'a very tall woman'. *The Universal Etymological Dictionary*, 3rd edn. Nathaniel Bailey, 1737.

Long Shanks: is a nickname originally used in reference to King Edward I, now it is applied to any tall man.

Loppus see *Lummox*.

Lord Muck: is a Cockney contemptuous term of reference to a person who puts on very fine airs and graces. There are numerous versions: Lord Monkey-Muck, Lord Muckety-Muck, Lord High Monkey-Muck, Lord Muck-a-Muck. The term, without the English Peerage title 'Lord', does the same duty in U.S.A. Mathews gives: 'high-muck-a-muck (2) A "big bug", a pompous person, . . . [and among the quotations]: "The professors—the high Muck-a-Mucks—tried fusion, and produced confusion." ' However, his sense (1) is 'Plenty to eat', and he states: 'Chas. J. Lovell in *Amer. Sp.* April 1947 pp. 91ff. has traced this term to its source in the Chinook Jargon. He has shown the prevalence of the two elements in the word, *hiu*, plenty, a lot, and *muckamuck* [or *mucamuc*], food, to eat. . . .' Its 'big bug' use in U.S.A. may indeed be a logical following from such an origin but it is not reasonable to suppose that it has influence in England. The origin is almost certainly in *muck*, dirt, rubbish, anything disgusting, cattle-dung.

Lost Lawrence see *Muttoned*.

Lottie: the almost inseparable nickname for any man named Collins. Formed on the name of the famous music-hall actress.

Louis (Louie): is the R.A.F. nickname for a Flight Lieutenant. From the American pronunciation *Lootenant*.

Louisvillains: is the general nickname used in the U.S.A. for natives or inhabitants of Louisville.

Lubber see *Lummux*.

Lucy Lovecock: is a Cockney nickname for any girl who is observed to associate with boys and young men. A girl does not need to be immoral to earn this nickname—the London 'lower classes' are painfully respectable and strait-laced in spite of their habitual profanity and bawdyness. The pun is double: Lucy—Loose.

Luff: is, in the American Navy, a nickname for a Lieutenant.

Lugs: is the inevitable nickname of anyone having protruding ears, but Flaps is not unknown.

Lummux: is an American nickname for a bulky, awkward, blundering person. Sometimes it is rendered, Lubbux, Lubber, Loppux or Loppus: all these forms are probably altered from Yiddish Lobbus, a fool: it occurs in the Jewish parody on Casabianca:

> The boy stood on the burning deck,
> His father called him 'Lobbus',
> Because he wouldn't wash himself
> And go to School[1] on Shobbus[2].

Lump-of-Lardy see *Jumbo*.

[1] Synagogue.   [2] The Sabbath.

Lumpy see *Jumbo*.

Lunk (shortened from *Lunkhead*): is employed in U.S.A. as a nickname for a stupid person.

Lushington (often preceded by Admiral, Alderman, Charlie, Johnnie, Mr., etc.): is a term of reference to a habitual drunkard. First recorded by Pierce Egan in *Boxiana* (1821). Barrère and Layland (1897) give '. . . up to recent date there was, or may be now, a tap-room in a certain hostelry in the immediate vicinity of Drury Lane Theatre, famous for being a favourite haunt of Edmund Kean. Here that ill-starred genius and his parasites were wont to turn night into day, in making their followers free of "The City of Lushington".' The hostelry was the *Harp Tavern*; 'The City of Lushington' a group (or club) of hard drinkers. The Chairman was the Lord Mayor, and each 'ward', namely, Juniper, Poverty, Lunacy, Suicide, was presided over by an Alderman. The word is derived from *lush*, 'wet', compounded with terminal 'ington', as many surnames have; for example, Washington—Harrington.

Lusty: is an American nickname for a cheerful, agreeable person.

M

Ma (pronounce *Mah*): is a general English, but particularly Cockney, term of address to one's mother; it is an abbreviation of *mamma*, which, being a natural utterance of young children, ranks as Standard English. It is common to numerous languages, and can be traced to Ancient Greek. It is a friendly and respectful form of Cockney address to any woman of matronly appearance: in the world of the theatre it has been the nickname of the keeper of 'theatrical lodgings' for about a hundred years. At some Public Schools *ma* (pronounced *may*), is used in place of 'major' and *mi* (pronounced *my*), in place of 'minor' to distinguish between elder and younger brothers, or boys of the same name.

Mab: is a nickname that from *c*. 1550 to *c*. 1850 was bestowed upon a prostitute.

Mac (or **Mack**): a general nickname for any Scotsman. From the 'Mc' prefix of so many Scottish names. It is also an Irish prefix, but the Irish characteristic is 'O'. *Mac*, 'son of' is both Scottish and Irish, but 'O', 'grandson of' is peculiar to Irish names. It is also a friendly term of address to a stranger, and in this usage has no Celtic significance.

Macaroni: nickname applied by British troops to Italian soldiers. 'Eyetie', generally in the plural, referred to the entire Italian nation, and the old friendly Cockney nickname, 'Jack' (Ice-cream Jack) was set aside for duration of war. It has now been revived.

Macky-moon: is a nickname given in the West of England to a fool.

Madame Cadenza: is an American radio producer's nickname for any female vocalist.

Madame La Zonga: is an American radio producer's nickname for a female performer who fidgets nervously before the microphone.

Madamoizook: is an American nickname for a French prostitute.

Maddy: is, in Scottish dialect, a nickname given to a fool. In the North of England it takes the form of *Madlin(g)*.

Mad-head see *Beetroot*.

Madlin(g) see *Maddy*.

Maff: is a nickname given, in the North of England, to a fool. Sometimes rendered *mafflin(g)*.

Mag (pronounce *Madg*): is a term of reference used in the Police Force, for a Magistrate.

Maggit: is the Cockney pronunciation of 'maggot', and is a temporary nickname, used in factories and workshops by the men, and given to adolescent boys who are suspected of 'galloping the maggot': that is, masturbating.

Magnus Tubus see *Jumbo*.

Mahogany: shortened form of 'mahogany knob', general nickname for a man with auburn hair.

Major: is the term of address, used by all ranks, to the Regimental Sergeant Major: it is almost a title.

Maltee: is an American general nickname for any person from Malta.

Malts: is one of the inevitable nicknames of any Maltese seaman.

Mama Lucia: is an American radio producer's nickname for a fat contralto.

Man John see *Mass John*.

Manc: is a general nickname given to natives or inhabitants of Manchester, and to boys at Manchester Grammar School. From *Manc*unian.

Maniac: is an American nickname for a person from Maine. Punning *Maine-iac*.

Maorilander see *Enzedder*.

Mardy: is a nickname used in the Midlands for a selfish and disagreeable, quarrelsome person. 'Mardy' is a dialect word meaning *marred*, spoiled. Those who attract the nickname have been spoiled children.

Maren: nickname for those members of the W.R.N.S. who served with the Marines: formed by telescoping *Marine* W*ren*. Also rendered *Marenette*. They wore the Marines' cap-badge instead of an H.M.S. tally ribbon.

Marenette see *Maren*.

Mark(s): is the inevitable nickname of any man named Spencer. From Marks & Spencer, once

'the originators of Penny Bazaars' (long years before Woolworths broke out at sixpence), now the place where penurious society women get their 'Bond Street' gowns.

Mars-bar: is noticeably usurping the place of *Chocolate* [q.v.] as the nickname of a 'coloured' boxer. *Mars-bar* is the name of a type of sweetmeat consisting of 'core' covered in chocolate.

Mary: is one of the inseparable nicknames of a man named Knight. From *nightmare*. It is also an inseparable nickname for any man named Hook, the reason not being clear. It is also a Cockney form of address to any little girl (under, say, fifteen) whose name is unknown: for example, a coster-monger will say, 'Yes, Mary—what can I get for you?'

Mass John: is a nickname for a Roman Catholic; used in Ireland. Its currency has spread, in a slightly altered form, to both Scotland and the North of England where, variously spelt, miss-, mess-, mex-, and man-, it is applied to a priest.

Master: a nickname that has become a formal mode of address to the Master-at-Arms.

Matchstick see *Skinnigut*.

Matchy see *Skinnigut*.

Maunsel: is a nickname given to a dirty, slatternly woman. It is also used as a term of reference. Yorkshire dialect.

Mawdy: is a dialect shape of *Mardy* [q.v.].

Mawmooin: is a nickname for both a simpleton and a teasing, tom-boyish girl. It is Yorkshire dialect, literally 'mow the moon'.

Maw'r: is a term of address to any girl, but is likely to become the nickname of a big, clumsy, awkward girl. Norfolk and Suffolk dialect chiefly, also Essex. Sometimes rendered *Mawsey*.

Mawsey see *Maw'r*.

Maypole: a nickname sometimes bestowed upon a tall thin person.

Mazlin(g): is a nickname for a feeble-minded person. North of England dialect: from Old English *maze*, delirium, or delusion, a state of bewilderment, confusion of mind.

Mealyface see *Zambuk*.

Measlenob see *Zambuk*.

Meg: is a general nickname for a countrywoman: cf. *Hodge*. In combination it has many dialect uses, among these is *Meg-Harry*. The reference is to a masculine woman, but there is no suggestion of this form being used as a nickname.

Mess John see *Mass John*.

Metzel: is a nickname given to a German in U.S.A.

Mex: is a nickname used in U.S.A. for a *Mexican*.

Mex John see *Mass John*.

Mi see *Ma*.

Mickey: is a nickname given by Cockneys to a 'tats' man; a picker-over of dustbins—a tramp who does no tramping, a collector of rags, bones and bottles who lives in his own idea of luxury on a few pence a day. [It is noteworthy that so long as these people do not 'take liberties', costers and other Cockneys are very kind to them in a rough way.]

Mickey Mouse: nickname for a *motor mechanic*: from Walt Disney's cartoon character. Originally naval in usage, now general. The Navy has retained *Motor mech.*

Mick(s): more often used in the plural than in the singular, the term refers to the entire Irish nation, or to the population of Irish ghettoes in big cities. It is always a term of reference, even in the singular: 'He's a Mick'. It is seldom employed now as a nickname, but before 1914 was inclined to be used for any Irishman in the Navy.

Microbe see *Midge*.

Middy see *Snotty*.

Midge (and **Midget**): is a nickname given to any person who is considerably below average in stature: when, however, a person is so extremely small as to be able to earn money as an 'exhibit', he or she falls into a category apart, and though correctly described as a midget, is not so nicknamed. It is probable that *Midge*, as a nickname, refers not to one who has failed to grow normally—a midget—but to the gnat-like fly, *Chironomidae*.

Iona and Peter Opie, in *The Lore and Language of School-children*, on pp. 169–70, under the sub-heading 'Little 'uns', say: '. . . Tich [q.v.] in a friendly manner, or "squirt" or "little squirt" in a less friendly manner. Alternatively: ankle-biter, dolly mixture (after a species of very small sweet), dumpy, flea, half-pint, imp, Jenny (in Scotland), junior [q.v.], kipper, microbe, . . . nipper [q.v.], penguin, pint-size, Pip, poached-egg, Shorty [q.v.], shrimp [q.v.], small-fry, snitch or snitchy, squib, squit (thus also Anstey in 1889, "he's not half a bad little squit"), stubby, stumps, stumpy, squiddy, twinkle toes . . . tiddler, tiger, Tiny Tim, Tom Thumb, tot, and, very common, weed. Also, inevitably, lofty, longshanks [q.v.], Goliath, etc.' Note that humour by inversion is known to children.

Midnight: is a nickname given by workmen to one who is slow, and unable to get a job finished in the normal time.

Milky: is the inseparable nick-name of any man named Watson. It appears to have originated in, and to be mainly employed in, the Army. It is also a term of address to the milk-roundsman:

which usage seems confined to Cockneys.

Mippet: is a nickname given to a very small child: partly a term of endearment, it becomes a nickname when it is retained in later life. Lincolnshire dialect.

Miracle-man see *Enos*.

Misery-gut: is a nickname earned by pessimists, and de-pressing people: it is also given to those who are critical of other people's mode of enjoyment.

Miss Anne: is an American negro's nickname for a white woman.

Miss Buttinski see *Buttinski*.

Miss John see *Mass John*.

Miss Hotbot see *Hotbot, Miss*.

Miss Lovecock see *Lucy*.

Miss Nancy: is a term of reference (obsolete by *c.* 1914) to one in a middle-class family of sisters, often the eldest, who refused her share of household duties, and insisted upon occupy-ing herself with 'lady-like' pur-suits: needlework, for example. In current use it refers to an effeminate man, or to a catamite.

Mister Charlie: is an Ameri-can negro's nickname for a white man.

Mocha (pronounce *mok-a*): is an American nickname for a negro—coffee-coloured.

Mochalie (pronounce *mok-a-lee*): is an American nickname for a Chinaman. Possibly a diminutive of Mocha, and im-plying not quite coffee-coloured.

Mockey: is an American nickname for a Jew. Possibly from *moccas*, sores, one of the plagues of Egypt, used by vulgar Jews as a curse: 'Oy—moccas on the momser.' Recorded by Daimon Runyon.

Mog: is a general nickname given to a girl named Margaret. *Meg*, which is virtually the same, ranks as a name in its own right, and as a diminutive, but not a nickname. The same may be said of *Peg*.

Mogga(er): is the inseparable nickname of any boy named Maurice. Evolved at juvenile level it remains to be seen whether it will survive into adulthood.

Moggy: is a friendly and affectionate nickname, exclusively Cockney in usage, for a kind, good-natured, unselfish girl. In the Midlands it has a very different meaning—it is there a term of reference to a slattern. It is also the inseparable nickname of any man named Morgan. Possibly a further obliterative change of *Molly*, itself perhaps suggested by the late XIX C. music-hall song:

Molly O'Morgan
With her little organ . . .

It is also frequently bestowed upon a native of Cheshire; moggie, a cat.

Moke: is an American nickname for a negro. Not connected with British *moke*, a donkey, but probably merely a shortening of *smoke* [q.v.]. Mencken, quoted by Mathews says: '*Moke* was thrown into competition with *coon* in 1899 by the success of "*Smokey Mokes*", a popular song . . . but is now heard only seldom.'

Molly: is a generic nickname for a girl, and is either bestowed upon, or else assumed by, the average prostitute. It is also a nickname for a married man who is so effectively managed that he spends his Saturday afternoon doing the housework: a henpecked man.

Mollygrub: is a general nickname given to a peevish, irritable person. From dialect mullygrumps, colic or stomach ache hence, bad temper.

Momser: is a term of reference to, and a general nickname for a high-spirited, lively boy. It is, or it would be, exclusively Jewish were it not for the fact that Cockneys, in intimate association with Jewish traders, pick up a great deal of Yiddish. The true meaning of the word (as a word) is *bastard*, but in Jews' usage it is as flexible as 'bastard' is in Cockney usage.

Mona: is a nickname given to a woman who is perpetually complaining: punning 'moan' from a radio character, Mona Lott. (The nickname is not applicable to moaning ladies whose name is Mona—they don't need it.)

Monkey-face: is, according to I. and P. Opie, a schoolchild's nickname for one having a 'funny face'. The term, used by adult Cockneys, is not a nickname, but a deliberate insult: ''Oo you lookin' at?—Monkey faice!'

Monkeynip see *Nip*.

Monsure: is a nickname applied to a Frenchman. It is a Cockney distortion of *monsieur*. In other parts of the country, and in U.S.A., the word is distorted to a local shape, but it is widely used.

Mopp, Mrs.: is a term of reference to, and a nickname for, any charwoman. From the name of the estimable 'charlady' who expressed her desire to do Tommy Handley now, in the war-time broadcast, ITMA.

Moppet: is a dialect shape of *poppet* [q.v.].

Mort Wop-apace: 'a Woman of Experience, or very expert at the Sport'. *The Universal Etymological Dictionary*, 3rd edn., Nathaniel Bailey, 1737.

Mose: is an American nickname for a negro. Possibly from the Biblical name, Moses. The negroes, in their simple piety, often choose names from Holy Scripture.

Moss: is an American nickname for a negro. The racial 'peppercorn' hair being enlikened to moss (Stonecrop).

Motor: is a nickname which may be, or may become, an 'inseparable' for anyone named Carter. Its use seems for the time being to be confined to London schoolboys, more particularly South London, perhaps most particularly South-East London. From contrast; *motor* vehicle, horse-drawn *cart*.

Motzas: is a jocular nickname for a Jew, from the Jewish term for the unleavened bread (biscuit) used at Passover. In use in Stepney, Hackney and other 'Jewish' London areas early XX Cent. Its usage has spread to U.S.A.

Mouchy: is the inseparable nickname, in the Army, of any man named Reeves. It is also an American nickname for a Jew, possibly from *Moisha*, the Yiddish form of 'Moses'.

Mr. or **Mrs. Buttinski** see *Buttinski*.

Mr. Clutterbuck see *Clutterbuck*.

Mr. Lo: is an obsolete general nickname for an American Indian. From Pope: 'Lo! the poor Indian, whose untutored mind. . . .'

Mr. Nonesuch see *Nonesuch, Mr.*

Mrs. Hitler see *Hitler*.

Mrs. McKenzie: is an American shop-assistant's nickname for a woman who habitually comes in, has all the stock down, and buys nothing. From the Yiddish *Mie ken zie*, 'I know her'. Another nickname given to the same type of nuisance, is *Mrs. Shome*, 'Show-me'.

Mrs. Mopp see *Mopp, Mrs.*

Mrs. Shome see *Mrs. McKenzie.*

Mucko: naval nickname for a stoker: from muck—dirt—the stoker's being a very dirty job.

Muddy: is the inseparable nickname of any man named Waters or Walters, or Waterson.

Mudhead: is a general nickname current in U.S.A. for anyone from Tennessee.

Mug: inseparable nickname for any man named Potts. Apparently Cockney in origin and usage. Sometimes rendered *Mugger, Muggie, Muggo* or *Mugs*. It is also often given to an ugly man. The addition of a final 's', which is becoming more common, seems to be an import from U.S.A. From 'mug', an earthenware cylindrical drinking-vessel hence, a *pot*.

Mugger see *Mug*.

Muggie see *Mug*.

Muggo see *Mug*.

Muller: is a nickname used only in the Brigade of Guards, for a German. From the common German surname.

Murph: is a general nickname for any Irishman in U.S.A. From the Irish surname Murphy.

Mush: the inseparable nickname in the Army since *c.* 1920 for any man named Knott: from the Arabic word for *not*.

Muskrats: is a nickname used in the U.S.A. for natives of, or inhabitants of, Delaware.

Muttoned (Mutton head): is a nickname given to a person who is habitually late. Probably from the rapidity with which mutton-fat congeals. It is also applied to a stupid person. From the dull intelligence of a sheep—duller when it has become mutton.

Iona and Peter Opie in their entertaining book, *The Lore and Language of Schoolchildren* (1959) give, on p. 366, under the sub-heading of *Latecomers*: 'To everyone but the teacher, he who arrives behind time causes a welcome diversion. "Ah! Here comes lightning!" [q.v.]. "Come on Christmas!" "The prodigal son has returned at last." "Here comes the late Mr. ——." "Better late than never!" "Better late than never, but better never late!" "You're a budding late bird." "Well rolled up." "You're early, what kept you?" "You want to wake up in the morning." "You'll be late for your own funeral." "You're too slow to catch a cold."

'He is a—Creepy-crawler, Cow's tail ("You're like a cow's tail, always behind"), Dilly-day-dream, guard's van [the last vehicle in a railway train], Idle-back, Lardy [this seems to link up with the idea of congealed mutton fat], Lazybird, Lazybones, Lost Lawrence, Sleepy Eyes,

Sleepy Head, Slowcoach [q.v.], Sluggabed, Snail.

'Lowsley's *Berkshire Words*, 1888, has: "Sluck-a-bed, sluck-a-bed, Barley Butt, yer yead be zo heavy 'e can't get up." This was recorded earlier, and in cruder form, in *Tommy Thumb's Pretty Song Book*, vol. ii, 1744, p. 34. In Ray's *Proverbs*, 1670, appears a jeer: "The sluggards guise, loath to bed and loath to rize." '

Mynheer Closh see *Closh*.

N

Nabby: is a nickname used at Brighton College for a master, who skilfully 'nabs' offenders against the rules. At Bushy Royal Masonic School the word *Tecker* is used with precisely the same meaning. Both defined by Morris Marples, in *Public School Slang*, 1940.

Nancy: is the inseparable nickname of men named Dawson. The tune 'Nancy Dawson' was the naval 'pipe' to draw rum rations.

Nanny (pronounce 'Nanah'): is the nickname bestowed upon a child's nurse. In the better-class family Nanny, who at the age of about eighteen was engaged to take care of the first baby, remained in employment to take care of each new arrival; she often took over the first baby of her first charge, and at the age of about eighty was herself being taken care of. Superannuation Scheme? National Insurance? No. Affection, gratitude, family pride and the honour of a gentleman worked better than either. In more humble families *Nanny*, reduced to *Nan*, is the nickname for the Grandmother (who often acts as nurse): a rhyming formation on *Granny* —*Gran*—itself reduced from 'Grandmother'. Nanny is a shape of *Annie*, and as a nickname for any serving-maid can be traced back to the early XVIII C.: from late XVII C. to about mid-XIX C. it was also the nickname for a prostitute.

Nark(er) see *Flatty*.

Narrow (pronounce 'Narrer'): is a favourite Cockney nickname for a thin man who need not even be tall with it.

Narrowback: is an American term of reference to an Irishman.

Nasty-face: an aggressive nickname given to any unfriendly or disagreeable person. Cockney, early XX C., probably from *Jack Nasty Face*, a common sailor, which can be traced back to the XVIII C.

Nat: is a nickname given to a very small man: also to one of a very bad temper. Scottish and Irish dialect. Probably the same word as *gnat*.

Natter-Knob see *Flatty*.

Navvy: naval nickname for the Navigating Officer.

Nazzy: is a North of England dialect nickname for a person of ill-temper.

Nebby: is a Scottish and North of England dialect nickname for an inquisitive person. From *neb*, the nose; hence, equivalent to *nosey*.

Ned: is the inseparable nickname of any man named Kell(e)y. It is of Australian origin and usage, recorded by Sidney J. Baker in *The Drum*, 1959. From the name of the famous Bush Ranger. It is also an English dialect nickname for a simpleton: short for Neddy, a common name for a donkey. In the West of England *Neddy Beecham* is a term of reference to a fool.

Needle: is one of the inseparable nicknames of any man named Cotton.

Needle-legs see *Skinnigut*.

Needles see *Skinnigut*.

Nellie: is the inseparable nickname of any man named Wallace (Wallis): from Nellie Wallace, the Lancashire Lass of the music hall; it is also an alternative for *Daisy* [q.v.].

Nena: is a dialect nickname for a fool.

Newfie: a nickname of American origin for a native of Newfoundland.

Newt: is a nickname given to a fool. Used chiefly by American taxi-drivers. From 'neutral', the gear position of a stationary vehicle.

Nic Frog: is an American nickname for a Dutchman.

Nick: is the inseparable nickname of any man named Carter. From 'Nick Carter', the famous detective of the 'penny bloods', c. 1875 to c. 1914.

Nigger: is the inseparable nickname of any man named Brown: it is also a general nickname for a man having a dark complexion, or particularly dark hair.

Nip: a nickname, of American origin, for a Japanese. From *Nippon*, the native name for Japan. In U.S.A. it sometimes becomes decoratively *Monkeynip*.

Nipper: is a general nickname likely to be given to any lively, likeable boy, particularly one of small stature, and once given, sticks to him for life. It was the nickname of the late Lupino Lane. The word meant a cutpurse in the XVIII C., but in XIX C. was used by the gangs of navvies for the boy who travelled with them to run errands, and from here it seems the general nickname has developed. A child of either sex may be referred to as 'a' or 'the nipper', but it applies particularly to a male.

Nippy: is a nickname for

any waitress: from *nippy*, quick, lively, efficient. The term was introduced in 1924 by J. Lyons & Co. Ltd., to characterize the waitresses then employed in Lyons' Tea Shops. Notwithstanding that the terms is Lyons' Registered Trade Mark it has, like other trade marks, become so firmly established that no one now recognizes proprietary rights —it is almost a standard substitutional word for waitress.

Nobbler: is a general nickname likely to be given to any popular person who does not qualify for a special one. 'Nobbler and Jerry, the Bloomsbury burglars', were a popular comedy pair (probably descended from 'Tom and Jerry') in the first decade of XX C. Originally the word referred to the confederate of the thimble-riggers.

Nobby: the inseparable nickname of any man named Clark, Clarke, Ewart or, by mispronunciation, Hewett. It is derived from the slang word *Nob*, the head from *c.* 1690: possibly a diminutive of *nob*ility, hence one at the head of affairs, hence a gentleman, or person of education. *Nobby*: pertaining to the nobs: any person or thing of a superior type. During the XIX Cent. the least enviable worker was the clerk; he was paid no more than an artisan (perhaps less than a skilled craftsman) but was expected to 'keep up

appearances' by wearing the black coat uniform crested with a top-hat. A clerk was, therefore, in appearance 'one of the nobs', hence, Nobby Clerk. The transfer on to Ewart is naval in origin. Admiral Charles Ewart was known as 'Nobby' on account of his dapper and smart appearance; hence, in the Navy, Nobby is also the inseparable nickname for any person named Ewart, or Hewett. The following anecdote is from a private letter written by Wilfred Granville, 2 March 1960: ' "Nobby" Ewart was Captain of the *Melpomone*, a "spit and polish" merchant *par excellence*. His time was the Med. Fleet in 1859–62, and yarns about him are legion. He had a private stock of poultry, and used to be extremely peeved when they were not fallen-in for Rounds or Divisions. The rating in charge got himself "in the rattle" over his neglect to keep the birds clean, so afterwards he painted the birds, and fell them in on a plank by means of tacks through the webs of the ducks' feet and a staple across the toes of the chickens.'

It is also a term of address to, and a nickname for, any person whose name is unknown. This usage seems to have emerged *c.* mid-XX C.

Nobby Coles, see *Knobby*.
Nocky: is, in the Army, an inseparable nickname for a man

named Knight. Nocky is a late XVIII to early XIX C. slang (from dialect) word meaning silly, hence there may be a punning inference: soldiers sometimes behave in a foolish fashion at night when in possession of an 'out of barracks pass'. In U.S.A., 'Nocky boy', shortened to 'Nocky' is a general nickname for one of inferior mental powers. It is American in its currency, but may have a British dialect ancestry.

Noisy: a naval nickname for any man who is of a retiring disposition, or who is taciturn. Humour by inversion.

Nonesuch, Mr.: is a disparaging nickname thrust upon a conceited person—one who thinks that *none such* as he exists: from the place name, Nonsuch, near Epsom, Surrey.

Noodle: was a nickname for a private in (or a member of) The Northumberland Yeomanry or Volunteers. It survives as a tolerant, and semi-affectionate, nickname bestowed upon a perfect ass, in society.

Norman: is the inseparable nickname of any man named Conquest. This surname, although uncommon, is probably met more frequently than *Pharaoh*. In Berkeley Gray's thrillers the hero, named Conquest, is called Norman.

Norsker: nickname for a Norwegian sailor. Used chiefly in the Merchant Navy. It is sometimes rendered *Norskey*.

Nosey: is the inseparable nickname of any one named Parker. Not likely to have been in use before the second decade XX C. Based on next entry, *c.* 1910.

Nosey Parker: is an aggressive nickname and a cautionary term of reference. 'Oi, mate, you want to fix them curtains o' yourn—every time ol' Nosey Parker Smith [Brown, Jones or Robinson] passes your 'ouse 'e slows deahn.'

Nosher: is a Cockney nickname for one who continually eats between meals. From Yiddish *nosh*, a delicacy.

Notty: is a general nickname for a native, or an inhabitant, of Nottingham.

Novy: is a nickname used largely in U.S.A. and also at sea, for a native of Nova Scotia.

Nozmo: is the inseparable nickname of any man named King. From the frequently displayed, and equally as frequently ignored, notice 'No smoking'.

Nozzer: is a temporary nickname given to a new arrival at a Naval Barracks. (H.M.S. *Ganges*, Shotley). From his repetition of 'No sir'. (Recorded by Wilfred Granville.)

Number One: the First Lieutenant: Royal Navy.

Nun see *Abbess*.

Nunky: is a familiar and

friendly Cockney rendering of *Uncle* [q.v.].

Nutty: is the inseparable nickname of any man named Cox. There may be in this seeming pointless combination a very subtle point indeed: *nuts*, the testicles; *nut*, the glans penis;

Cox is homophonic with *cock(s)*, the penis. It is also a nickname for anyone who takes a large size in hats, or who is inclined to show a preference for 'highbrow' entertainment: from *nut*, the head.

O

Oaste: was a nickname given by the merchants to strangers who came to Newcastle to buy coal.

O.C. Grease: is a nickname applied to the Sergeant Cook. Popular during the 1914–18 war, when 'O.C.' (Officer Commanding), and 'O.i.C.' (Officer in Charge) was applied to as many functions as the soldier filled: *O.C. Swills*, one engaged on salvage: *O.C. Latrines*, *O.C. Crap* (and other variants), one engaged on sanitary work.

Ofay: is an American negro's term of reference to a white man. Wentworth and Flexner believe it to be centre-slang (which they term 'pig-Latin') on *Foe*.

Okie: is a nickname for a native of Oklahoma.

Olaf: is a general nickname for a Swede. From the popular Swedish given name.

Old Bill: a 'character' created during the First War by Bruce Bairnsfather, whose *Fragments*

from France helped to keep us smiling. Until *c.* 1925 it was a term of reference used by all classes, for any man with a 'walrus' moustache. It is now very seldom heard.

Old Horse see *Horse, Old.*

Old Man, The: is, in the Royal Navy, a term of reference to the Captain: in the Merchant Navy to the ship-master (who is not a 'Captain' unless he achieved that rank in the Navy): in the Army, to the Commanding Officer: in civilian life to one's father, or to one's employer, and in all four worlds it is often rendered, 'The Old 'Un'.

Old Shaver see *Young Shaver.*

Old Toast: 'a brisk old fellow'. *The Universal Etymological Dictionary*, 3rd edn., Nathaniel Bailey 1737.

Old-top see *Horse, Old.*

Oldster see *Younker.*

Omaloor: is a term of reference and a nickname for any person with disproportionately big feet. It is used in U.S.A. and

4

Canada, but is unknown in Britain and Australia.

One: naval officer's term of address to the First Lieutenant: cf. *Number One* of which this is an abbreviation. *One O* is a First Officer W.R.N.S.

One Ringer see *Ringer*.

Onion (sometimes **Spanish Onion**): is a nickname given to an amusing, lively fellow. Cockney in origin and usage: now obsolescent. Perhaps the idea is a pungent delicacy (?) that may bring tears to the eyes!

Oomick: is a Scottish dialect term of reference (and nickname for) used jocularly, to a very small person, particularly a child; from Old Norse *ormr*, a worm.

Ord: a naval term of reference to the rank of Ordinary Seaman.

Orderly Buff: a military term of reference to the Orderly Sergeant.

Orderly Dog: a military term of reference to the Orderly Corporal.

Orderly Pig: R.A.F. nickname for the Orderly Officer.

Orderly Stooge: a term of reference applied to an Orderly Officer or N.C.O. Military, and seems to have been evolved to cover Officers, Sergeants, and Corporals, when the Orderly Pig, Buff and Dog began to become confused.

Organ-grinder(s): is a general nickname used for Italians. It was first employed for the 'Gari-baldi refugees', fell from popularity, was revitalized in 1914, again in 1939, and is still alive even though inactive.

'Orris (or **Horace**): shortened form of 'Horatio' is, in Royal Naval usage, the inseparable nickname of any man named Nelson. In the City of London, in the commercial offices but not in the banks, it is a term of address and a nickname for a young male clerk. Cockneys, particularly Costers, use it as a term of address to any nice, polite, neatly attired young man with whom they make contact: 'Pahnd av-apples? Yhus 'Orris!'

Oscar: is a term of reference to, and a nickname for, a man who is suspected of active homosexuality. From the name of Oscar Wilde, whose literary fame is overshadowed.

Ossie: is an alternative, largely American, spelling of Aussie [q.v.].

Oven: is a nickname sometimes bestowed upon a man having an abnormally large mouth—the inference is that it can house the whole leg of mutton with room to spare. It was, of course, never more common than the feature, and is now seldom heard.

Owner, The: sometimes applied to the Captain of a ship, but generally to members of the public visiting. The term is said to originate from a person having gone aboard a new battleship and asked for the captain, saying, 'Tell him one of the owners would like to look over the ship.'

P

Pa: a Victorian 'genteel' nickname for one's father: an abbreviation of *Papa* from Latin *Pater*, Greek *Pappas*, 'father'. The word lost caste on the expiration of the XIX C., and *Dad*, which can be traced back to 1500, came into its own again: reduplicated to *Dada*, it is at least two hundred and fifty years old, but *Daddy* seems to belong to the XX C. The U.S.A. shape of *Papa* is 'Popper' hence *Pop* [q.v.]. It was also a nickname bestowed upon a Parish Relieving Officer in the days when such functionaries existed.

Paddy: a nickname bestowed upon any Irishman. It is far more commonly used than Pat, probably because the latter, a diminutive of Patricia, is a favourite feminine given name. In Australia it is given to a Chinaman. (Sidney J. Baker.)

Paddy Webster: nickname given to an inefficient seaman. Evolved *c.* 1840. From the name of a crimp in Liverpool who, under pretence of shipping experienced seamen, supplied lubbers.

Paleface: is an American-Indian's term of address and nickname for a white man. It is also used jocularly by one white man to another. *Big White Chief*, an allegedly Indian term, is similarly employed. Reduced to 'Pale' it is used in the same way by American negroes.

Palmetto: is an American nickname for a native of South Carolina: from the palmetto tree emblem of the State.

Pants: is the nickname given by stewards to the pantry-man. Passenger liners. Dave Marlowe, *Coming Sir!* 1937.

Pape: is used in U.S.A. in reference to a Roman Catholic: from Papist.

Paraffin Pete: is an R.A.F. nickname for the Officer in Charge of airfield control: one of his most important duties being that of ensuring the timely and adequate illumination of the flare-path.

Parleyvoo: is a nickname sometimes used both in Britain and U.S.A. for a Frenchman.

Pat see *Paddy*.

Patess: is a term of reference used in America for an Irishwoman.

Patch: nickname for a man who has developed a bald patch at the crown of the head.

Patlander: is a term of reference to an Irishman in U.S.A.

Paul Pry: term of reference to an inquisitive person: from the title role in the play *Paul Pry* by John Poole—played in 1853. The term, which is sometimes rendered *Peter Pry*, is a favourite with Cockneys in whose estimation a man's first virtue is his ability to mind his own business.

Paul's Pigeons: is a nickname for boys of St. Paul's School. It was mentioned by John Stow 1598. Paul's Pigeons fought in the street with St. Anthony's Pigs and ultimately (it would seem) exterminated them, for St. Anthony's School did not survive.

Pavement Pounder see *Flatty*.

Pay: nickname for the Paymaster Lieutenant, evolved *c.* 1914. Naval only.

Paybob: is the naval rating's nickname for the Accounting Officer.

Pea Crackers: is a term of reference, used by Yarmouth fishermen. It includes the entire population of Lowestoft.

Pealer see *Peeler*.

Pea-nuts: is the inseparable nickname of any man named Phillips.

Pea-soup: is a nickname used in U.S.A. and Canada for a French Canadian, from the idea that such soup is their sole diet.

Peckerwood: is a nickname given in U.S.A. to anyone from the Deep South. It is often shortened to *Peck*.

Peckle: is the nickname given in the West of England to an itinerant entertainer, a conjurer or clown. Local shape of *Pickle*, itself short for *Pickle herring*. 'Pickle, an arch waggish fellow; Pickleherring, the zany or merry andrew of a mountebank,' *Lex. Balatronicum*. See also Joseph Addison, in *The Spectator*, No. 572, 1714.

Pedlar: is the inseparable nickname of any man named Palmer. From the name of the pugilist. The following suggestion is too 'highbrow' to be acceptable: a Palmer was a Pilgrim; Pilgrims, on their return from the Holy Land, sometimes became pedlars of portions of the One True Cross in the genuineness of which merchandise some of them may even have believed.

Peeler: is one of the inseparable nicknames of any man named Murphy. It is also a term of reference to a Police Constable from the surname of Sir Robert Peel, who introduced, in 1814, *The Peace Preservation Act*, and later, *The Metropolitan Police Act*, under which Police Forces were appointed. In the U.S.A., where it may be spelt Pealer, it is a nickname that may be applied to a person of either sex who displays extraordinary energy, or to any Irishman. It is assumed, because many Irishmen have become policemen, that the term is transferred from a constable (Irish or not) but the route is quite a different one. The commonest nickname for a man named Murphy is *Spud* which is slang for potato—one has to *peel* a potato hence *peel a spud—peeler spud Murphy.*

Peewee: is a nickname given in U.S.A. to any short man. It is also used for undersized animals.

Peg see *Meg.*

Peggy: is the inseparable nickname of any man named Legg. This, unlike most inseparable nicknames, was, during the Second War, used also by girls in the various branches of the Service. It is often reduced to *Peg*. It is also one of the inevitable nicknames for a man with one leg, and though it is derived from the old type of wooden 'peg-leg', it survives in this age of undetectable artificial limbs. It is, further, a nickname for an effeminate man: chiefly in Lancashire.

Pegpuff: is a nickname given to a girl, or young woman, who pretends to maturity and experience beyond her years. Scottish and North of England dialect.

Pelican: a general nickname sometimes given to a man from Louisiana, U.S.A.: from the Pelican-in-her-Piety, the armorial bearings of the State Governmental body.

Pelt: is a nickname, or term of address, of a jovial character, used in the North of England. It may be applied to any man; 'Come, my old Pelt—have a stingo!' It is the same word as *pelt*, a hide or skin.

Pen: is a nickname given in Scotland to 'an old saucy man with a sharp nose'. (Quotation from E.D.D.) It probably refers to 'an old man with young ideas', one who makes sexual overtures to girls and young women. (Cf. the Cockney phrase, used when a man or boy has 'woman trouble'—'He should learn to keep his pen in his pocket.')

Penamites: one of the nicknames applied to the inhabitants of Pennsylvania, U.S.A.

Pencil-slim see *Skinnigut.*

Pengun: is a nickname given to a loquacious person, from the fact that he 'cracks [talks] like a pen-gun'. *Pen-* or *pop*-gun, made from the tubular wingbone of a large bird, charged by pressing into a potato (or turnip) and fired by forcing the vegetable disc down the tube with a ramrod. Used as a bird-scare in various English counties.

Penguin see *Midge.*

Penny: is the inseparable nickname of any man named Singleton. From the name of Penny Singleton, the film star—about 1945.

Penny loaf: nickname current in the XIX C. among thieves to stigmatize an honest man: one who would rather live on a penny loaf than on stolen beef. J. Redding Ware in *Passing English*.

Pensy: is a nickname given to a quiet, thoughtful, sedate girl: one who is pensive. North of England dialect.

Pen-y-Liggen: is the nickname given to a ne'er-do-well young man who, after having left home to seek his fortune, returns without having found it. Sometimes rendered *Peter Lacken*, and probably derived from 'penny lacking'. Cf. the rhyme:

Owen Moore went away
Owing more than he could pay.
Owen Moore came back today,
Owing more!

Peola: is a nickname given by American negroes to a light-skinned girl of their own race.

Pepper: is an American nickname for a Mexican, from the strongly spiced native dishes of Mexico.

Pepper-pot see *Fireworks* and *Zambuk*.

Percy: is a nickname given in the Navy to a man of superior education, or one who is quiet, and fond of reading.

Peter: is a nickname given to a painter. From one referred to as 'Peter the Painter', who, it was alleged, escaped from the battle of Sidney Street, London, E.1, in 1910.

Peter Funk: is the nickname given, in XIX C., by auctioneers, but now by 'rings' of dealers to a man 'put up' to bid for a lot when a private buyer is present, so as to force the price up.

Peter Lacken see *Pen-y-Liggen*.

Peter Pipeclay: is a sailor's nickname for a Royal Marine, from the pipeclayed white belts.

Peter Pry see *Paul Pry*.

Pfumph: is a general nickname for anyone displaying curious mannerisms, or eccentricity of character. From the self-revealed name of the 'sinister figure' whose mission was to thwart Tommy Handley's activities in the war-time broadcast, ITMA.

Phar Lap: is a term of address to a person slow in his movements. Usage confined to Australia from the name of a racehorse that became famous far beyond the Australian racing world in 1933, by being poisoned while on a visit to Mexico. The name means 'streak of lightning'.

Philadelphia Lawyer: is a general nickname for a man well versed in current affairs, level-headed, and able to give acceptable advice to perplexed neighbours. It is American in origin and can be traced to Colonial times. It originates in the Quaker Lawyers being supremely honest and reliable.

Philip: is an underworld nickname for a policeman. Eric

Partridge (*A Dictionary of Slang and Unconventional English*) says: 'mostly in "Philip! the police are coming . . ." possibly by a punning reference to *fillip*.'

Phillipean: an American nickname for any *Filipeen* woman.

Phizog: is a general nickname for anyone with rugged features: sometimes *Phiz*. Reduced from Physiognomy.

Phosgene: is a military nickname, evolved during the 1914–1918 war, for the Anti-Gas Instructor: from the name of industrial carbon-oxychloride, or chloro-carbonic acid ($COCl_2$), the 'standard' poison gas, first prepared by J. Davy, 1811. During the Second War it was revived for the Passive Defence Officer whose duties included anti-gas instruction.

Pickal: was the nickname given to a miller: from his *picking*, or dressing, the millstones.

Pickleherring: is an American nickname for a Dutchman.

Pie-can: is used by Cockneys as a nickname for a stupid person. In use during the first decade of XX C., and probably twenty-five years ealier. The stove trundled by vendors of hot pies was the 'can'.

Pig-bin see *Hungry-guts*.
Pig-hog see *Hungry-guts*.
Pig, small see *Small pig*.
Piganog see *Hungry-guts*.
Piggy: is one of the inseparable nicknames given to any man

named May: it is also the nickname given, in the Royal Navy, to the rating whose occupation is that of attendant on the Petty Officers' Mess.

Piker: is an American nickname for a native of Missouri, especially one from Pike County.

Pill: naval nickname for a Customs and Excise Officer. The inference is that he will turn everything out.

Pillar-box see *Jumbo*.

Pillick: is a friendly nickname used by Cockneys for one who is unwisely good natured: 'Nark it, Pillick, you've awready paid two rounds—let someone else 'ave a basin.'

Pill-stick: is a term of reference to the humorist of the party, or to any amusing person. Yorkshire dialect. Cf. the Cockney word *cure*, an amusing person: 'She's a proper cure, ain't she? Thought I'd 'a died!' [of laughter].

Pills: is the inseparable nickname of any man named either Beecham, or Holloway. From respectively, Beecham's Pills, 'worth a guinea a box', and 'Holloway's Pills and Ointment'; both popular remedies, the latter largely advertised on toilet rolls 'printed with clarified ink on non-irritant paper' and supplied either free, or at greatly reduced prices, to Borough Councils, who provided them in public lavatories. It is also the nickname used in the Army for the Medical Officer's orderly. His duties vary between floor scrubbing and issuing No. 9: in the Navy it is bestowed upon the Junior Medical Officer.

Pilot: is the nickname given in the Navy to the Navigation Officer.

Pimple: is a jocular nickname sometimes given to a man who takes an abnormally small size in hats.

Pimple bonce see *Zambuk*.

Pincher: inseparable nickname of any man named Martin. It originates in the Navy from the fact of Admiral Sir William F. Martin having been a strict disciplinarian who insisted upon ratings being put under arrest (pinched) for most minor offences. The family of Martin has given a number of brilliant Admirals to the Navy, notably William Martin (1696–1756) son of Commodore George Martin: Thomas Byam Martin (1773–1854): Sir George Martin (1764–1857). 'Pincher' Martin was C.-in-C. Mediterranean *c.* 1860. His brother, serving during the same period, was known as 'Fly' Martin from the name of his ship. This inseparable nickname is in general use, and has reached high social levels. 'Taffrail' (pseud. Henry Tarprell Dorling), used it for a book-title: *Pincher Martin, O.D.: a story of the inner-life of the Royal Navy* (1916). William

Golding published (1956) a novel also entitled *Pincher Martin*.

Ping: nickname, among naval officers, given to the Asdic Officer. It is echoic of his instrument. 'Asdic' is a word formed of the initials of *A*nti-*S*ubmarine *De*tection *I*nvestigation *C*ommittee. The same listening device used by the U.S. Navy is called *The Sonar Gear*.

Pinkerton: is the American equivalent of the British term *Sherlock* (or *Sherlock Holmes*). It is a nickname implying that the wearer is a shrewd, deep-thinking, farseeing fellow who, putting two and two together makes five before anyone else has noticed. From Allan Pinkerton who, in 1850, founded the famous 'Pinkerton's National Detective Agency'. In Scottish dialect, however, it is the nickname given to 'a person of small intelligence'. Mactaggart, *Encyclopaedia*, 1824.

Pinkie: is a nickname used in U.S.A. for a Mulatto.

Pint-size see *Midge*.

Pip see *Midge*.

Pipe-cleaner see *Skinnigut*.

Pipes: nickname for the bo'sun in the old Navy. The modern nickname is *Bose*.

Pippin: is a Cockney, friendly nickname by which almost anyone, from one's wife to the next stall-holder, may be known. It occurs as early as 1664: 'Thou'rt a precious Pepin . . .' Cotton.

Pisan: is a nickname given by Cockneys to a boaster, or to one who uses threats. From *piss-and-wind*: (in full, 'He is all piss and wind').

Pisky: is a Scottish term of reference, applied to members of the Episcopalian Church.

Piss-pot jerkers: an uncomplimentary term of reference, used by deck-hands, to describe Cabin Stewards in passenger ships.

Piston: is a nickname given to an Engineer Officer. All Services.

Pixy: is a nickname given to a dainty, graceful little girl: it is inclined to remain with the person when womanhood has destroyed daintiness, and grace is gone. From *pixy* or *pixie*, a West of England dialect name for a fairy.

Pizzy: is a nickname for a mischievous child. Scottish dialect.

Plates: nickname for those engaged for washing-up in a passenger ship.

Player's (Please): generally the first word only, but sometimes both together is the nickname for any man in the Navy who, having obtained 'permission to grow full set', achieves the robust growth and picturesque appearance of the bearded seaman who for many years has been the 'hall-mark' of Player's Navy Cut Cigarettes. (Men of

good taste spend sleepless nights worrying lest, in these streamlined plastic days, John Player should 'modernize' his advertisement.)

Plodderoner see *Enos.*

Plum-pudding see *Jumbo.*

Plumber: is the nickname of a Royal Naval Engineer Officer. It has no reference to 'a pipe spoiler', a plumber, whose nickname is *Plummy*, but is a humorous pejorative: a warship's engines are called *plums.*

Plummy see *Plumber.*

Poached-egg see *Midge.*

Podge: a general nickname for a fat person. Sometimes rendered *Podgey*, or *Podger(s)*. Eric Partridge, in *A Dictionary of Slang . . .* gives: 'a short, fat person; such an animal: dial[ect] and coll[oquial] from *c.* 1830. . . . a nickname from *c.* 1840.' Also rendered, *Podger* and *Podgey.*

Pokerface: is a nickname given to a person who hides his emotions: keeps a 'straight face' under all circumstances. Not, as is often supposed, from the straightness of a poker, but from the necessary facial control exercised by a player of the card-game so named.

Pollyanna: is an American nickname for a cheerful, high-spirited girl. From a character in the fiction produced by Mrs. John Myman Porter (1868-1920).

Polygamists: nickname of the inhabitants of Utah, U.S.A. (So

4*

recorded by John S. Farmer in *Americanisms, Old and New*, Privately Printed, 1889.)

Pommy: an Australian nickname for a 'new chum' from England. For origin see Eric Partridge, *A Dictionary of Slang and Unconventional English*, p. 646.

Pompey: is a nickname given to an undersized boy. North of England dialect.

Pong: is a nickname given to a Chinaman in Australia—punning the *ong* sound in some Chinese words, and *pong*, a bad smell.

Pongo: is a nickname given to either a soldier or a Marine by a sailor. It is from the conventional name by which a showman addresses a performing monkey.

Pony: inseparable nickname for any man named Moore. From 'Pony' Moore of the Moore and Burgess Minstrels. *c.* 1885.

Pooky: is a dialect nickname for a fat person.

Pop: is a nickname bestowed upon any man who is of mature years in a community of younger men. It was not employed in the Services until the Second War, and is of American origin. During the 1914–18 war *Dad*, or possibly *Uncle*, would have been used. There is a modern tendency for youth to use it in the home for 'Father' (if he will stand for it!), but its use is more deliberate than spontaneous.

Poppet: is, in mid-XX C., acquiring the status of a nickname that may be given to persons of either sex or of any age, but always to people who have pleasant manners, or endearing qualities. The word, which is standard English, originally meant a doll (now *Puppet* has assumed that speciality). It later (XVII C.) referred to a small or dainty person, even to a dwarf; later it was attached to a charming young woman, or to a female child. In early XX C. it became a term of endearment for the female, later for either sex. Now it is a general nickname and on the road to becoming slang.

Poppy: is the most popular of the three inseparable nicknames that become attached to the name Tupper. The other two are 'Shovie' and 'Sticky'.

Popularity Jack see *Jack Shalloo*.

Porker see *Jumbo*.

Porky: a friendly jocular nickname for a Jew. See also *Jumbo*.

Porridge see *Jumbo*.

Posty: a Cockney form of address to the postman.

Potty: is a nickname given to a fat boy at St. Bees School. From *pot*-bellied.

Pouncer: was the nickname used during the Second War for a fire-watcher. He (or she) pounced on incendiary bombs.

Powder: is the inseparable

nickname of any man named Horn(e). In the *Evening News* (1959–60) a strip-cartoon Western appeared in which a character named Horn featured and he was called 'Powder'. From the horn used to carry gunpowder in the days of muzzle-loading guns.

Poxie see *Zambuk*.

Pricker, the chief: a nickname for the Regulating Chief Petty Officer, Stokers. H.M. Navy only.

Pricky: is a nickname used in the Navy for any man who seems to be in need of a tag, and whose surname neither has, nor suggests a new, inseparable. It is an amusing transition of the well-established Cockney 'Cock' [q.v.].

Professor: is the inevitable nickname of any man who has, or who pretends to, a superior education, or a specialized knowledge of any particular subject. It appears to be particularly Cockney in its usage, but the Cockneys are shrewd enough to distinguish between those who possess, and those who merely pretend to, and on this dichotomy depends whether it is employed in a complimentary or in a derisive spirit.

Props: is the nickname of the property-man in the theatrical world, both in England and U.S.A.

Prune: is the nickname given

in the R.A.F. to a Pilot Officer who takes unnecessary risks. It is an American nickname for a fool.

Pruneface: is an American nickname for a smile-less person. From the name of a popular strip-cartoon character.

Prune-picker: is an American nickname for a native or an inhabitant of California.

Pud see *Jumbo*.

Pudding-pie see *Jumbo*.

Pudd'n'ed (Pudding head): is primarily a descriptive term for a fool, and occasionally it is a nickname for one: but it is often transferred by Cockneys and attached to the 'pretty-pretty' feminoid male. It is an appropriate nickname for such since the typical expressionless, characterless countenance resembles strongly a boiled suet pudding.

Puke: is a nickname used in U.S.A. for a native of Missouri. Mathews says, 'The reason for this application of the term is not known, cf. Irish *puke* "a poor, puny, unhealthy looking person" . . .'

Punch: is a general nickname for a short, thick-set man.

Pussy: is the inevitable nickname of the elder of two brothers at King Edward's School, Birmingham.

Pussyfoot: is a now obsolete nickname for a campaigning teetotaller. From 'Pussyfoot' Johnson, the American 'do-gooder', who, like all his kind, did incalculable harm.

Putty: nickname employed in the Navy for the ship's painter.

Q

Q see *Queue*.

Quack: is a nickname (not subject to interpretation) for a doctor. Services and Cockney. It is a friendly nickname, applied to one's Panel Doctor in whom one has the utmost confidence. It does not carry an implication of lack of knowledge or lack of skill in either diagnosis or treatment.

Quarter(s) see *Queue*.

Queen Bee: is a term of reference used in the R.A.F. for the senior Woman W.A.A.F.

Queer Fellow, The: is a term of reference used in the Regular Army for the Officer-in-Charge irrespective of who he may happen to be, while O-i-C.,

he is 'The Queer Fellow (or Feller)'.

Queue (pronounce *Kwe-we*): is a term of reference to the Quartermaster Sergeant. Military usage, a development since the Second War, influenced by the influx of 'National Service' recruits. A development of 'Q', an abbreviation of *Quarter(s)* which itself was in use in the Army before 1914.

Quid: is the inseparable nickname of any man named Pound. Its usage seems to be confined to the Navy. Admiral Sir Dudley Pound was very wittily nicknamed Phoney Quid: from *phoney*, false, hence *dud*. Quid, a pound sterling (£1).

R

Rabbit: is the inseparable nickname of any man named Hutch, Hutchins or Hutchinson. Very rarely *Bunny* [q.v.].

Rack see *Wrack*.

Rackensack: is a term of reference to, and a nickname for, a native of Arkansas, U.S.A.

Raddie: is a nickname and a term of reference for an

Italian. Its use is confined to the underworld.

Raggie: Bluejackets' term for a close friend. It is equivalent to rhyming slang 'China' which, though rhyming on *mate* (China plate), carries a greater emotional content than does the word 'mate' itself. When two friends fall out, they are said to have parted brass-rags'. The sharing of these essential cleaning materials being the basis of the term. It is also a Scottish and North of England nickname for a dealer in rags and other forms of household lumber.

Raghead: is a nickname bestowed upon an Indian, or other Oriental who wears a turban.

Rags and Bones: term of reference applied to the Officer-in-Charge of salvage operations. Needless to say it has currency only during wartime. It does not ante-date the 1914–18 war.

Rainbow: is a nickname for a bandy-legged person.

Rajah: is the inseparable nickname of any man named Brook(e)s: from Rajah Brooks of Sarawak. (First white Rajah, Sir James—1841, third, Sir Charles Vyner, who ceded the territory to Britain in 1946).

Rake(y) see *Skinnigut*.

Ral: is the naval term of reference to the Admi*ral*.

Ramsammy: is a general nickname used in the West Indies, for a coloured labourer, or coolie.

Ramsey (or **Mr. Ramsey**): is a nickname given to a lascivious person. From *ram*, a male sheep whose abilities are proverbial.

Ranzo: nickname for any native of the Azores who served on a whaler: from the name Alonzo.

Rastus: is a friendly nickname for any negro, but particularly for one of advanced years.

Rat: was a nickname given to members of a local Religious Sect in Indiana, U.S.A., in mid-XIX C.

Rattler: inseparable nickname of any man named Morgan. It is derived from a dialect term *Morgan Rattler*, meaning first-class.

Ratto see *Doggo*.

Razor-blade see *Skinnigut*.

Razzo (pronounce *Rahzo*): is the inevitable nickname bestowed upon any man with a chronically red nose. In cold weather, anyone who has developed a temporarily red nose will be so greeted. ''Ullo Rahzo! Come in an' sit be [by] ne ole Anna Maria, an' meowt (melt—i.e. thaw) it aht!' The term was recorded as long ago as 1899 by Clarence Rook (in *Hooligan Nights*), who refers it to the nose irrespective of its colour but, even if it was correct to do so then (which is doubtful), it most certainly is not now: a nose that is not red is not a *Razzo*.

Red: nickname for an agitator: one who is habitually 'agin' the Government': who is perpetually declaring that someone 'ought to be put against a wall and shot': who attempts to stimulate a political argument even during a game of darts.

In America, though it sometimes means 'Communist', it often merely indicates auburn (red) hair, which was the earlier (British) usage: (see Somerset Maugham's story of that name).

Red Cap: a general term of reference in the Services for a Military policeman: from the red cap cover by which they can be identified.

Red Cape: a term of reference to a Sister in Queen Alexandra's Imperial Military Nursing Service. Evolved during the 1914–18 war.

Red hat: a general term of reference current during the 1914–18 period, to a staff officer.

Reddy see *Beetroot*.

Redhead: nickname of, and term of reference to, any girl with auburn hair, either of natural growth or artificially so coloured.

Red Kipper see *Beetroot*.

Red-mop see *Beetroot*.

Red-paint-brush see *Beetroot*.

Red-thatch see *Beetroot*.

Reefer: is a nickname and term of reference used in Australia for any person connected with the Great Barrier Reef.

Reelo: is one of the inseparable nicknames of any man named Cotton. From *Reel of . . .*

Reemee see *Reemy*.

Reemy (or **Reemee**): is the Army nickname for members of the Royal Electrical and Mechanical Engineers. Since 1942.

Reggie: a term of reference, but never of address, to the Regimental Sergeant Major.

Rib-skin see *Skinnigut*.

Rice-belly: a nickname for a Chinaman on the Pacific seaboard of the United States of America.

Richard: is a general nickname for a hunchback.

Rig see *Wrig*.

Riggin: is a nickname given to an abnormally tall woman. Scottish and North of England dialect: probably the same word as *Riggin(g)*, the spine.

Right-foot: is an American nickname for a Roman Catholic.

Ringer: in the Navy a general term for a Lieutenant: in the R.A.F. a one-ringer is a Flying Officer; a two-ringer, a Flight Lieutenant; a three-ringer, a Wing Commander; a half-ringer, a Pilot Officer; a two-and-a-half-ringer, a Squadron Leader.

Ringtail: is an Australian nickname for a person lacking courage. It was adopted by the American Navy, during the Second War, and applied to a Japanese.

Rip: is a nickname given in U.S.A. to one who is opposed to, or unresponsive to, modernization. From the name of Rip Van Winkle who, in Washington Irving's story, slept for twenty years.

Robert see *Flatty*.

Rocky: is the naval officer's

nickname for a Royal Naval Reserve Officer. It is also a general nickname for a boxer who can take punishment.

Rod: is a surveyor's nickname for his assistant: from his being the *Rodman*, i.e. the main part of his business is to handle the surveyor's rods.

Rodney: is a nickname given to a lazy, idle person. North of England and Midlands dialect.

Roineck: is one of the nicknames used in U.S.A. for an Englishman.

Rok: is an American Army nickname for a native of South Korea; from *R*epublic *o*f *K*orea.

Roly-poly: is a nickname for a short, plump man, and a term of reference to a woman of similar build: it enjoys both British and American currency.

Rom: is the nickname for the *R*adar *O*perator-*M*echanic. Current in the R.A.F., but not unknown in other Services where radar is employed.

Romyed: is a nickname given to a stupid, blundering person: from *Ram's head*. Lancashire dialect.

Rovers: nickname of the inhabitants of Colorado, U.S.A.

Rozzer see *Flatty*.

Rubberguts see *Jumbo*.

Rube: is an American nickname for a rustic: an agricultural labourer: equivalent to British *Hodge* [q.v.].

Rudolph: is a very recent nickname (and likely to prove an ephemeral one) for anyone with a red nose. From a popular song, 'Rudolph the Red-Nosed Reindeer' (1949).

Rufus see *Beetroot*.

Rum-Bottle: a general nickname for a sailor: from the naval issue of rum.

Rumble-tummy see *Hungry-guts*.

Rumps see *Buffalo*.

Russian: is a nickname given in the Northern States to a negro from the Southern States; a pun on *rush*, hurry: he is rushing (pronounce rush-un) away from hard work.

Russki: a term of reference to Russian soldiers during the 1914–18 war. Now applied to all Russians.

Rusty: is the inseparable nickname of any man named Steele. It was evolved in the Navy, where they know a great deal about the effect of sea-water on steel, and on other 'bright work', and is fairly obvious, but why it should equally be the inseparable nickname of men named Adams in the same Service does not appear. It is also one of the inevitable nicknames to which a man with auburn hair must answer, but it is not, as might be expected, a short form of Rusty-*knob*, or -*top*, but of Rusty ballocks and—in the Navy —it is very often employed in full.

Rustyguts: 'an old, blunt fellow.' *The Universal Etymo-* *logical Dictionary.* 3rd edn., Nathaniel Bailey, 1737.

S

Sage hens: nickname of the inhabitants of Nevada, U.S.A.

Sailor: a nickname bestowed upon all ex-seamen engaged in semi-public jobs—such as messenger to the Office of a Ministry. It is also likely to be thrust upon any man who walks with a rolling gait.

Sails: inevitable nickname for the sail-maker aboard ship.

St. Anthony's pigs see *Paul's pigeons.*

Sally Bee: is a not obsolete nickname for a tall, thin woman: from Sarah Bernhardt who was the tallest and thinnest woman ever to achieve stage success.

Salt Beef Squire: nickname for a naval Warrant Officer. Now obsolete.

Salt-horse: naval nickname for a commissioned officer with no special duty hence, one who may do, or be, anything about the ship except a specialist. From the salt beef—which might have been anything—that came out of the 'harness casks' of the old Navy.

Salts and senna: a term of reference, popular during the latter half of XIX C. applied to a doctor. It is now obsolete.

Sam: is the nickname generally bestowed upon a man from Liverpool. In American it is given to a university student who belongs to the *Sigma Alpha Mu* college fraternity.

Sambo: is a general nickname for any negro. Of American origin, and apparently traceable to the slave days. Imported into British usage via the Navy.

Sammies: a general, and temporary nickname used to describe the American troops during the 1914–18 war. When America 'came in' a newspaper enjoined the public not to call them 'Yankees'—another periodical suggested '*Sammies*, after their *Uncle*'. An American General said: 'If there's one name the American soldier dislikes, it's "Sammy".'

Sandy: is the inseparable nickname of any man named Brown, from the colour of sand: it is also a Thames waterman's nickname for any member of the crew of a dredge barge. It is also the nickname inclined to be used in address by a Scotsman to a fellow Scot, who is unknown to him, in which use it is the diminutive of Alexander.

Sandy Hooker: a New Zealand shepherd's nickname for

one of their own calling native of Nelson. Possibly from some now forgotten but once notorious character, or from an anecdote.

Santa see *Father Christmas*.

Sardine: is a nickname bestowed upon a boy who is undersized. It was in use among London schoolboys up to the First War, but now seems to be extinct: it was, too, the nickname of the Duke of Windsor when he was a Cadet at The Royal Naval College, Dartmouth, and it is a XIX Cent. American nickname for a sailor engaged in whaling: either by contrast, or from the cramped conditions for the crew aboard a whaler.

Sarg(e): a friendly form of address to a sergeant, the use of which demands tact since it is a little on the familiar side hence, not always suitable even on off-duty occasions. It is never used as a term of reference (Cf. Killick). The smart and soldier-like word is 'sarnt' prefixing the name: 'Sarnt Pardy is doin' the rounds.' Also 'Sarnt-Major'.

Sasso: is a term of reference applied to the Senior Air-Staff Officer.

Satch(el): is an American nickname for anyone with a large (physical) mouth, or a 'big' (metaphorical) mouth: that is, one who talks too much.

Sauerkraut: a nickname used for a German in U.S.A. From fermented cabbage, an article of German diet.

Sausage: was a nickname applied in the XIX C. to any German. The Denmark Hill, Camberwell, district was a German colony: there they set up a 'gymnasium' where, while passing themselves off as lovers of England, they were receiving Prussian Military Training and toasting 'Der Tag'.

Sawback: is a mis-spelling of *Sore-back* [q.v.].

Sawney: was, XIX C. and before 1914, a general nickname for a Scotsman. The 1914–18 war popularized *Jock* [q.v.] and *sawney* is now applied only to simpletons irrespective of country of origin. It comes from *Alexander* via *Sandy* [q.v.] and notwithstanding its Scottish origin is very popular in Ireland, and fairly common in England.

Scabby-guts see *Zambuk*.

Scandahoovian: is an American term of reference to, and nickname for, a Scandinavian. Mencken (*American Language*, 1937) gives: '*scandihoovian, scandinoovian, sowegian* [q.v.], *scowegian* [q.v.], *scowoogian, scoovy.*

Scandihoovian see *Scandahoovian*.

Scarecrow see *Skinnigut*.

Scaredy-cat see *Fraidy-cat*.

Schnozzle: is the inseparable nickname of any man named Durrant; from Jimmie Durante

(b. 1893) of film and radio fame. It is also bestowed upon one with a prominent nose.

School-dinners see *Zambuk*.

Schooley: Services nickname for the Schoolmaster—Navy, Army and Air Force.

Scoovy see *Scandahoovian*.

Scotland Yard: is a nickname for a police detective, or for a private detective: from the name of the street in which the Metropolitan Police Headquarters was originally housed.

Scouse: is the inevitable nickname of any man from Liverpool: from *Lobscuse*, a local dish. (According to some commentators it should be applied only to Liverpool-Irishmen.)

Scowegian: naval nickname for a Scandinavian. A blend of *Scandinavian* and *Norwegian*.

Scowoogian see *Scandahoovian*.

Scraggy see *Skinnigut*.

Scrappy: an old Cavalry nickname for a farrier.

Scratch: naval nickname for the Captain's secretary. Quill pens emitted a scratching sound in use, and steel pens, before the rounded point was introduced, did so to an even greater degree.

Scruffy: is applied as a nickname to any man who is habitually untidy. The word, meaning contemptible, inferior, dirty, is a XIX C. expression, possibly of schoolboy (Christ's Hospital) origin from *scurfy*. See Eric Partridge, *A Dictionary of Slang and Unconventional English*.

Scrufty see *Flatty*.

Scud: is a nickname for a running champion. Rugby School.

Scufter: is a nickname for a policeman. Scottish and North of England dialect. Formerly used very commonly in Newcastle.

Scurse: nickname used in the Navy for any man who tries but fails to qualify for *Players* [q.v.]: from Whi*skers*.

Scuttle: is a term of reference used by taxi-drivers in Chicago, for a negro 'fare'. The reference is probably to the blackness of coal which is stored in a scuttle.

Seal: is a term of reference applied in America, to a negro girl: the inference is smooth black skin.

Sec: nickname for either the Admiral's, or the Captain's, secretary.

Secret Harry: naval nickname for a senior officer's secretary: not only a pun, but an inference that he is in his principal's confidence—knows his secrets.

Seebee: nickname for men of the Royal Engineers working with the Royal Navy. From *Com*bined Operations.

Seedy: is an American nickname for a negro.

Senior: is a nickname and term of address employed in the Royal Navy for the Senior Engineer Lieutenant.

Sepia (or **Sepe**): is an American nickname for a Mulatto.

Sexton: is an American radio producer's nickname for a performer with a bass voice. Sexton —the digger of graves.

Sexton Blake: a military nickname for the Provost Sergeant: from the 'penny blood' weekly detective stories wherein Sexton Blake, his boy assistant Tinker, and the marvellous bloodhound Pedro, did miracles of criminal catching.

Shad: is a nickname given in America to anyone with a full, or protruberant, upper lip. Sometimes extended to *shad-mouth*: the implication is an overshadowed mouth.

Shadder: is a now obsolescent nickname for any thin man, from the Cockney pronunciation of Shadow.

Shade: is an American nickname for a negro.

Shag (or **Winlaton-shag**): is a nickname used in County Durham, for a native or an inhabitant of *Winlaton*.

Sham: is a nickname given to an Irishman in U.S.A. It is a shortening of *Shamrock*, which is sometimes used in full.

Shanghai: is an American nickname for a tall, thin dandy. It was current at the end of the XIX Cent. and is now obsolete. From the name of a long-legged fowl.

Shark(e)y: is the inseparable nickname of any man named Ward. Possibly from the name of a pirate, only too well known to the Navy, which was kept busy by him in West Indian and Caribbean waters. It is also attached to Armstrong: and is one of the nicknames bestowed upon a sharp-featured man.

Sheeny: in the Navy a nickname for any economical, or 'near' man: in civilian life, for any Jew.

Shevvie: is the general nickname of any man from Sheffield, Yorkshire.

Shilling see *Flatty*.

Shine: is an American nickname for a negro. Probably by inversion from the fact of his skin being dark.

Shiner: this was originally the inseparable nickname of any man named Bright. The connection is obvious. It soon became transferred to any man named Wright, because of the association of sound and the more frequent occurrence of that name. The same process was involved, in part, in its transference to the name White; but here an additional allusion to the shine of fresh white paint is operative. Humour by inversion transfers Shiner from White to Black. It is attached to the name Green because that is the colour of vert-de-gris which encrusts 'bright work', i.e. brass, copper, bronze and other basic yellow-metal fittings and fixtures aboard ship. All men named Bryant answer to Shiner, from 'shine a light', meaning direct the beam of a lantern, or ignite the ship's lamps, the source of which illuminant was a safety match manufactured by Bryant and May.

Shiney: a general nickname often given to a conceited person. Probably from the phrase 'He thinks the sun shines out of his arse.' It is also a variant of *Shiner* [q.v.].

Shitface: is a nickname that comes into temporary use on hilarious, drunken occasions and, strangely enough, is compliment- ary, being applied to good-natu- red, easy-going, likeable fellows: for example, ''Ere! Come on, ole Shitface, gis that song wot you know abaht, "'E Painted 'er"!' There was, too, the Cockney kid, conscripted on to a Charity Country Holiday, who sat by a stream and held a twig from which depended a length of string terminating in a bent pin. The local Curate, crossing the meadow, espying him, cried in a jovial, amiable manner, 'Hullooo—my young piscator!' and received the equally jovial, amiable response, ''Ellaow—me ole Shitface!' Cf. next entry.

Shitpot: is an aggressive nick- name, expressive of dislike and contempt. It is generally well merited, and the easiest way to earn it is to be the workshop tale-bearer.

Shitwig: is a nickname and term of reference used in con- tempt. Yorkshire dialect.

Shoey: one of the inseparable nicknames of men named Smith, from the farrier, or shoeing- smith. It was also a general nickname for farriers in the Cavalry.

Shome, Mrs. see *Mrs. McKen- zie.*

Shon(acker): is a nickname used, both in its short and long form, for a Jew in U.S.A.

Shonkey: nickname for a Jew, extended to any mean man.

Short-arse: occasional nick- name of, and general term of reference to, a short man. All Services, and in civilian life at several social levels.

Shorty: is the inseparable nickname of any man named Long, and of any man named Little, one of the inseparable nicknames of men named Wright and, by humour of inversion, the inevitable nickname of a tall man. It is also sometimes applied to a small man.

Shot: is an American under- world nickname for a negro who is 'in the rackets', or who is a professional thief.

Shovelpenny: is a military nickname for the Regimental Paymaster. It was in general use up to 1914 and at that period began to decline. It is now rarely, if ever, applied.

Shover: one of the many inseperable nicknames for men name Smith.

Shovie see *Poppy*.

Shrewdy: is seldom used as a nickname, but often as a term of reference to a Service 'smart Alec', a cunning fellow.

Shrimp: a nickname employed at several social levels for any man or boy who is below average size.

Shuffer: is a term of reference to, and a nickname for, a fat person. Cornish dialect.

Signals (sometimes shortened to *Sigs*): nickname for the Signals Officer, Royal Navy.

Sigs: Nickname for a signalman, also a term of reference. All Services.

Silver: is a nickname used in America for an elderly man with silver (white) hair.

Sinbad: Regular Naval Officers' nickname for officers of the Royal Naval Reserve.

Sis: is an American nickname for a sister. It now has a small currency here, but it is used consciously, and rather artificially.

Skates (**Skating Rink**): is a general nickname for a bald-headed man. The term seems to have originated in the Navy.

Skeate-gob: a term of reference of a reproachful character applied to natives of Allonby, Cumberland.

Skeck: is a nickname for 'a person of proud, disdainful, or pugnacious character. A policeman at Workworth was known as "Old Skeck"'. Wright.

Skelly: is a nickname used in Ireland for a man with a squint.

Skemmy: is a nickname bestowed upon a person in contempt—probably upon a severe person. Wright gives: 'At a school where I was, we had a boy from the North who nicknamed the headmaster Skemmy. When asked the reason he said that the master was like their vicar, and he was skemmy.'

Skibby: is a nickname given to any person of either sex or any age of Mongolian race and Japanese (not Chinese) origin. It is used exclusively on the Pacific Coast of America. Mencken (*American Language*) says it was originally applied only to a Japanese prostitute plying her trade in the States. In Scotland it is a nickname and a term of reference to a left-handed person.

Skillet: is an American negro's nickname for a member of his own race.

Skilligareen see *Skinigaree*.

Skin and bones see *Skinnigut*.

Skinbone see *Skinnigut*.

Skinflint see *Skinnigut*.

Skinigaree: is a term of reference to a thin person. Eric Partridge gives *Skilligareen*, which is probably merely an alternative form. See his *Dictionary of Slang and Unconventional English*.

Skink: a rather low-grade nickname for a waiter. American in origin, and employed chiefly in the underworld there.

Skinkin-ap-Morgan: is a now obsolescent general nickname for a Welshman.

Skinnigut (skinny gut): is one of the inevitable nicknames that Cockneys bestow upon a thin man.

Iona and Peter Opie give, in their entertaining book, *The Lore and Language of Schoolchildren* (1959), p. 168, under the subtitle of 'skinnies': 'bag-o'-bones, bean-pole, Bony Maroney (Glasgow), broomstick, daddy-long-legs, drain-pipe . . . fuse-wire, hair-bones, hairpin, lamp-post, walking-lamp-post, Lanky Liz, Lanky-Panky, Long and lanky [see *Lanky*], skinny and cranky, Swanky Lanky Liz (a character in *Beano*) [*Beano*, a coloured comic], L.S.D. (Long Skinny Davy), matchstick (sometimes abbreviated to "matchy"), needles, needle-legs, pencil-slim, pipe-cleaner, rake (very common— and medieval) [accompanied by a footnote quoting Chaucer's use—1387], or Raky, razor-blade, rib-skin, scarecrow, scraggy, skin and bones [with footnote giving American "skin-bone" and "string-bean"], skinny, skinny-flint, or skinflint (cur-

iously common in this sense), skinnyguts, skinny Liz, skinny-malink, spaggy or sparrow (one with long thin legs), Spindle Dick, spindle-legs, spindleshanks, spindle-sticks, taper, Thinima, (opposite to Fatima), tin-ribs, and, of course, such names as Tubby [q.v.]. . . .'

Skinny see *Skinnigut*.

Skinny-and-cranky see *Skinnigut*.

Skinny-flint see *Skinnigut*.

Skinny Liz see *Skinnygut*.

Skinny-malink see *Skinnigut*.

Skipper's doggie: nickname for a Midshipman acting as the Captain's A.D.C.

Skippy: when employed by white men in U.S.A. it is sloven pronunciation of *Skibby* [q.v.] but when employed by negroes it is a nickname for an effeminate man.

Skips: an uncommon nickname for the Captain (R.N.) or the Master Mariner (M.N.).

Skowse: is the inevitable nickname of any seaman who comes from Liverpool.

Sky: is a nickname given in Australia to an Italian immigrant. (Possibly because Italians cannot refrain from talking of the beautiful sky of Italy.)

Skylon: a nickname given by children to a lanky boy. From the ugly and senseless erection that helped to increase the financial disaster of 1951 known as 'The *Festival* of Britain'. I and P.

Opie, in *The Lore and Language of Schoolchildren* (1959) point out that its use has spread as far from London as Ruthin.

Skyscraper: a nickname given by children to a lanky boy. Recorded by I. and P. Opie in *Lore and Language of Schoolchildren* (1959).

Slant: is a nickname used in U.S.A. for a person of Mongolian race. Short for *slant-eye*.

Slasher: is the inevitable nickname of any man who suffers from a weakness of the urethral sphincters: from to slash (or to have a slash), to urinate, hence the nickname is applied to one who continually breaks off an occupation, or a conversation, to obey the call. In Ireland it is a nickname bestowed upon natives and inhabitants of Cavan: from Miles O'Reilly, Prince of Brefuie, who was known as 'Miles the Slasher of Ballinagh'. In the Irish usage it refers not to mituration, but to slash, to cut, hence to fight lustily.

Slave see *Enos*.

Sleepy eyes see *Muttoned*.

Sleepyhead see *Muttoned*.

Slen: is short for *Slender*, a general nickname for a tall thin man.

Slide: is the inseparable nickname of any man named Overett. Notwithstanding that this surname is uncommon, the Navy was not prepared to let such an opportunity pass.

Slider: is one of the inseparable nicknames of a man named Cross.

Slim: is a nickname given in Canada to anyone named Callaghan, but in the Royal Navy it is the inevitable nickname of a fat man.

Slinger: an inseparable nickname of any man named Wood(s). It is current chiefly in the Army where 'a slinger' is a term applied to bread, dumplings, or sausages floating in potable liquor (from tea to soup). The connection may be that wood floats on water.

Slob see *Jumbo*.

Slodger: is a nickname given to a native of the Fens. Lincolnshire and Norfolk dialect.

Slogger: is a nickname given to a hard-hitting fighter. With professionals it becomes a sort of by-name: as, for example, 'Young Slogger Smith, the flyweight wonder'.

Slop see *Flatty*.

Slopie: is an American nickname for one of Mongolian race—probably from the apparent slope of the eye. Not in use before the Second War.

Slottie: is a Scottish nickname for a postman. Iona and Peter Opie, in their valuable book, *The Lore and Language of Schoolchildren* (1959) record 'Slottie Johnnie' as a nickname for a postman in Aberdeen.

Slowcoach: is a general (an obvious) nickname for a person of sluggish habits. It is also applied, by the humour of inversion, to a person who is abnormally quick.

Sluck-a-bed see *Muttoned*.

Slug see *Jumbo*.

Slugabed see *Muttoned*.

Smallfry see *Midge*.

Small pig: is a term used by ratings to describe a Petty Officer.

Smallocks: is a nickname given to a small, spare person. Yorkshire dialect:

'Fattocks and Smallocks wor laikin at taw

Fattocks ga'e Smallocks a bat ower t'jaw;

Smallocks ran home to tell his mother,

Fattocks ran after, an' gav' him another.'

Smidget: is a nickname given to a negro in Mississippi, U.S.A. Harold Wentworth, in *American Dialect Dictionary* (1944) says: 'perhaps a blend of *smidg*in [plus] *midget* or smicket'. It is, apparently, a negro word.

Smig: nickname applied to the *S*ergeant-*M*ajor *I*nstructor of *G*unnery. Naval.

Smigget: is a nickname bestowed upon a regular-featured, conceited man, who regards himself as God's gift to the fair sex. It is a term seldom heard outside of the Navy, or the Island of Malta, G.C., hence the supposition that it is a standard Maltese word. It is not. It is probably derived from *smicket*,

an English dialect word meaning a woman's intimate undergarment, and itself sometimes applied, as a nickname of contempt, to the same type of man, for they are found in all walks of life.

Smiler: is a general nickname for a person who lacks a sense of humour, morose, or habitually depressed (and depressing!).

Smitty: is one of the numerous nicknames attached to Smith.

Smokey: is the inseparable nickname of any man named Holmes. Eric Partridge suggests (*A Dictionary of Slang and Unconventional English*, p. 798) from 'smoky homes' (i.e. defective flue). In U.S.A. it is one of the nicknames applied to a negro.

Smokey Joe: nickname for the Officer in Charge of 'make-smoke' operations. In the London Fire Brigade which was, before nationalization, the best in the world, and was largely manned by ex-naval ratings, *Smokey Joe* was the nickname of any member of the 'Breathing apparatus' (a kind of diver's helmet!) crew.

Smouge see *Smudger*.

Smouky: is an endearing nickname for a young male child. Scottish dialect.

Smudger: substitution for Smith, and employed chiefly in the Navy. It is sometimes pronounced 'Smouge' or 'Smudge'. To smouge is to deceive, or 'wheedle' or cadge. There is no direct connection, merely a fortuitous similarity. Smudger is from smudge, to soil or smear, by the soot floating in a blacksmith's shop.

Smusch: is a general nickname, used in Scotland, for a short, dark, hairy person.

Smutty: is the inseparable nickname of any man named Black.

Snail see *Muttoned*.

Snake: is an American nickname for a native of West Virginia.

Snakey: inevitable nickname for a thin man. Naval in origin, but used also in civilian life. Often rendered '*Snako*'.

Snap: is a nickname given to a pert youth. Yorkshire dialect.

Sniffy: is the inevitable nickname given by Cockneys to anyone who behaves as though he has a perpetual cold in the head, but considers a handkerchief to be only a decoration for the outside breast-pocket. Among outdoor workers there are many who answer to this nickname: some of them suffer from hay-fever, most of them merely from habit.

Snip: is the inseparable nickname of any man named Taylor: from to snip (cut) with shears, hence a slang term for a tailor. It is also the inseparable nickname of men named Parsons, possibly from a phonetic con-

juring trick, Parso*nip*, Par*snip*; i.e. the root of umbelliferous *Paetinaca Sativa* which primitive man mistook for an edible substance—a mistake that has persisted into modern times.

Snitch(**y**): is one of the inevitable nicknames thrust upon a person having a prominent nose. From *snitch*, the nose, a low slang, or underworld term of XVIII C. origin.

Snobber: is the nickname given in the Navy to each individual member of a 'snobbing firm'. (Group of ratings who mend shipmates' shoes). See also *Flatty*.

Snook or **Schnook**: is a nickname used by Cockney Jews for an inquisitive person. From the Yiddish for 'nose'.

Snoops: is the Service nickname for a R.A.F. policeman.

Snooser: is a nickname given to a person of Scandinavian origin in U.S.A.

Snotty: a general nickname for a Midshipman: from, some naval wits suggest, that when the Lords of the Admiralty ordered a row of three buttons to be attached to the cuff of a full-dress round-jacket, it was to prevent the sleeve being used as a pocket-handkerchief. The Navy's 'Young Gentlemen' are themselves amused by the nickname, and they keep it alive with greater success than they achieve in their endeavour to kill 'Middy'—so beloved of maiden aunts.

Snowball: nickname bestowed by the American Forces on their own Military Police: from the hemispherical helmet the M.P.s found it advisable to wear. The name was adopted by British Forces, and on the international exchange some distortion occurred hence *Snowdrop* and *Snowflake* may both be encountered as alternative forms. In the British Navy the term has a separate existence, being the nickname of a man with fair hair, and in U.S.A. civilian circles, of a negro.

Snowy: is an inseparable nickname for any man named Baker. The reference is to the sprinkling of flour with which a baker is coated during working hours: cf. *Dusty*. It is also the nickname, by the humour of inversion, for any man who has dark hair or complexion; and for a tall man, the inference is that snow remains on mountain peaks.

Snozzle: is an alternative spelling of *Schnozzle* [q.v.].

Snuff: is a nickname for a negro. Used in Texas, U.S.A.

Soapy: is the inseparable nickname of men named Hudson, or Pears, or Watson: from the names of these famous brands of real soap (not chemical detergent). Soapy Sam was the nickname of Bishop Wilberforce: b. 1805, became Bishop of Oxford in 1845 and developed an unctious manner. The nickname had come into general use by c. 1860, and remained his till his death in 1873.

Sodger (soldier): a term of contempt used as a nickname for a lazy, good-for-nothing messmate. It is employed in both the Royal Navy and the Merchant Navy, and to some extent among dock-workers. It arises out of the old Navy's attitude towards the Marines.

Soo: is the naval nickname of Staff Officer Operations.

Sooner: is an American nickname for an Australian.

Sore-back: is an American nickname for a native of Virginia.

Sowegian: is an American term of reference to, and a nickname for, a Scandinavian. It may have a punning reference *sow*, female pig, and *sou'*, sloven pronunciation of 'South', itself inverting *Nor'* (North) in Norwegian.

Spade: is one of the nicknames applied in U.S.A. to a negro. From *Spades*, a black suit in a pack of playing cards. Spades in preference to Clubs (also black) probably because in fortune-telling by cards spades indicate ill-luck, and a negro in U.S.A. certainly has plenty of that. The term is slowly being adopted in Britain, and was used by Teddy-boys c. 1947.

Spaggy see *Skinnigut*.

Spaghetti: nickname for an Italian, used in both Britain and U.S.A. but in the latter country it is frequently abbreviated to *Spag*—or *Spig*.

Spaginzy: is an American nickname for a negro. Probably a perverted form of *Spade* [q.v.].

Spanish Indians: nickname of the inhabitants of New Mexico, U.S.A.

Spanisher: is an American nickname for a Spaniard.

Sparks: in the Merchant Navy, a nickname for the Wireless Operator. In civilian circles, a nickname for any electrician. In the Royal Navy the wireless operator is called *Sparker*.

Sparrow see *Skinnigut*.

Spick: is a disparaging nickname for a Mexican, anyone of Latin race, or anyone with a swarthy skin. From 'Me no spick-a da lang.' Said to be their invariable excuse for anything. It might, however, be a form of *spig* or *spag*.

Spider: is the inseparable nickname of any man named either Webb, or Kelley. It is also a nickname for anyone with disproportionately long legs and arms.

Spig see *Spaghetti*.

Spike: rhyming on *Mike*, short for Michael, has been a nickname for those named after the Archangel, for more than a century. It is also the inseparable

nickname of any man named Sullivan. Eric Partridge says, in *A Dictionary of Slang and Unconventional English*, Sullivan was the name given by tramps when they went to a casual ward in an area where Irish potato-hoers were working. The casual ward was called 'the spike' because of the hardness of the beds, the food, and the treatment. Another possible origin is from the name of the famous prize-fighter. It is also the inseparable nickname of any man named Hughes. It is given by Cockneys to tall thin men, and in this context it was in use in the last quarter of XIX C.: perhaps even earlier.

Spinach: is a nickname used in U.S.A. for a Spaniard.

Spindle Dick see *Skinnigut*.

Spindle-legs see *Skinnigut*.

Spindleshanks see *Skinnigut*.

Spindle-sticks see *Skinnigut*.

Spitfire: is a general nickname given to an aggressive person of either sex.

Splinter: is one of the inseparable nicknames for any man named Wood.

Spokey: is the inseparable nickname of any man named either Wheeler, or Wheelwright. The reference is, of course, to the craft of wooden wheel construction, which is all but killed by the motor industry where discs of stamped iron are good enough.

Spongey: is one of the

inseparable nicknames of any man named Baker. Perhaps from sponge cake.

Spot (Spots or **Spotso):** is an inevitable nickname for a youth in the throes of an attack of acne: when the condition is rectified the nickname is abandoned. (Sometimes he is called *Spotty Dick*).

Sprat: is a nickname given to a lively but undersized person. From *Jack Sprat* (?) of no-fat-eating fame.

Springbok: descriptive of a soldier (also a civilian) from South Africa.

Spud: is the inseparable nickname of any man named Murphy, the occasional nickname of any Irishman, and sometimes a term of reference to a particular Irishman as: 'He's a regular Spud Murphy, isn't he?' Both 'Spud' and 'Murphy' are slang terms for potatoes. Every Irishman named 'Murphy' (and there is a large number) says the term originates from the fact of the first plantation of potatoes in Ireland having been on land held (or formerly held) by the O'Murphy sept.

Spunk-dust: is a friendly term of address which may be used in the convivial atmosphere of a pub (or elsewhere) by any man to any man.

Squarehead: a general nickname for any German. Originally Australian for any immigrant,

later for a German immigrant, now obsolete in Australia but current in British English.

Squasho: is an American nickname for a negro.

Squatters: nickname of the inhabitants of Dakota, U.S.A. (so recorded John S. Farmer in *Americanisms Old and New*, Privately Printed, 1889).

Squelch see *Enos*.

Squib see *Midge*.

Squiddy see *Midge*.

Squinny-guts: is a term of reference to, and a nickname for, a thin, miserable, complaining sort of a person. South of England dialect, but apparently related to *Skinny-guts*.

Squire: a semi-complimentary term of address to a stranger, favoured by Cockneys. Its usage is as old as this century, and may extend back into the latter part of the XIX.

Squirt see *Midge*.

Squo: nickname applied to a W.A.A.F. Officer equal in rank to a Squadron Leader. Official title, *Squa*dron Officer, hence the name.

Staff: term of reference (sometimes of address to a Staff-, a Colour-, or a Quartermaster-Sergeant, Military: to a Staff-Nurse, Hospitals.

Staffy: nickname for a Staff Officer, naval.

Stanshaw Nannygoat: is a term applied in the Navy to a bad-tempered man.

Steady: during the Second War it was an inseparable nickname for any man named Barker, but it has not survived. Wilfred Granville in *Sea Slang of the Twentieth Century* gives ' "*Steady Barker!*" a catch-phrase from the Navy's radio revue *Merry-go-Round* featuring Eric Barker. A popular show during the 1939-45 war.'

Steam Bo'son: a naval term of reference to an Artificer-Engineer.

Steam-Roller see *Jumbo.*

Steve: is the inseparable nickname of any man named Donoghue, and also for Donovan, which is a more common surname. From the famous jockey.

Stewpot see *Enos.*

Stick-in-the-mud: is a term of reference to, and a nickname for, an unenterprising person. It was in use as early as 1733.

Sticker: is the inseparable nickname of any man named Leach (or Leech).

Sticks: nickname for a drummer, or, in the Navy, a bugler. Military in origin, but annexed into civilian life and used largely in the jazz (and other) band circles. It is also a nickname bestowed upon a man with one leg quite irrespective of the mechanical perfection and total invisibility of his artificial limb, and not even demanding his use of a walking-stick.

Sticky see *Poppy.*

Stilty: a nickname given by children to a weedy boy—the inference is that he is walking on stilts. Recorded by I. and P. Opie in *Lore and Language of Schoolchildren* (1959).

Stitch: is an inseparable nickname for any man named Taylor.

Stitcher: a nickname sometimes given to the Sailmaker.

Stodge: is a nickname for a fat person. Scottish dialect.

Stokehold Boson: naval nickname for the Warrant Engineer.

Stokes: is a naval nickname for a stoker. It came in with coal, and went out with the influx of oil.

Stonethrowers: a nickname used in Ireland for the inhabitants of Tipperary.

Stonewall: is the inseparable nickname of any man named Jackson: from Thomas Jonathan Jackson, Confederate General, 1824-63, himself so nicknamed.

Stormy: is the inseparable nickname of any man named Gale. Even if nicknames were not customary, in the Navy this one would surely be irresistible.

Stott: is a nickname for a young, awkward, gangling sort of person. From the North of England dialect word *stott*, a young ox or horse.

Stranger: is a general mode of address, used particularly in the Western States of America. Its inclusion among nicknames seems questionable, but it has as much claim to that status as had *Bud* [q.v.].

Streak: a nickname given by children to a lanky boy. Recorded by I. and P. Opie in *Lore and Language of Schoolchildren* (1959). Adults—especially Cockneys—use it as a term of reference: 'Long streak of whitewash' or—the less polite—'of piss'.

Stream-line: a general nickname for any tall man. Possibly of R.A.F. origin.

String-bean see *Skinnigut*.

Striper: a naval term of reference for Officers: Two-striper, a Lieutenant; Two-and-a-half-striper, Lieutenant-Commander; three-striper, Commander. The term is applied chiefly by officers. Ratings are more inclined to use *Ringers* [q.v.].

Stripey: nickname for an Able Seaman. Naval in origin and usage from the arm badge accompanying the rank. It is sometimes applied to a Sergeant of Marines for the same reason.

Stroppy: nickname for a trouble rousing hand, a *Jack Strop*, a sea-lawyer: from the word 'obstreperous' mis-pronounced *obstropulous*, and shortened to *strop*. Stroppy's *Raggie* [q.v.] is called 'Jack Strop's Old Woman'.

Stubby see *Midge*.

Stud: is a nickname given to a lascivious person.

Stum: is a nickname given to a deaf and dumb person in Irish dialect. Strangely enough, a word having almost the same sound, *shtum*, is Yiddish for a deaf mute. As racing-slang, *a shtumer*, a horse that is a certain 'also ran', it can be traced into XIX C.

Stumps see *Midge*.

Stumpy see *Midge*.

Sub (or **Subby**): nickname for a Sub-Lieutenant in the Royal Navy, and for the second in command at a London Fire Brigade Station before the Second War.

Sucker: a general nickname used in U.S.A. for anyone from Illinois: but its more common usage is for a dupe.

Sue: a naval nickname for *S*taff *O*fficer Operations: formed from the initial letters. Sometimes so written—i.e. *Soo*.

Sugar: is the inseparable nickname of any man named Cane, Cain, or Kane.

Sugar-baby: is an Australian Army nickname for members of the Australian militia.

Sukey: a general nickname for a servant-girl. Now obsolete.

Sunny: is the nickname given to a habitually cheerful person. Sometimes extended to *Sunshine*, and also *Sunny Jim*: the latter from an advertisement for a patent foodstuff. In U.S.A. the first and second are used ironically for a habitually depressed person.

Swabian (or **Swarby**): is a derogatory nickname applied to a German. It is used in Poland and other states adjacent to Germany. *Dictionary of International Slurs*, A. A. Roback, (1946).

Swaddie: term of reference and general nickname for a private soldier. Originated in the Navy, early XIX C. from dialect: a clod-hopper, or country-bumpkin. Before the end of the XIX C. it was in general use.

Swanga Buckra see *Bukra*.

Swank: is the inseparable nickname of any man named Russell. (From the rustle of a 'swanky' gown?).

Swanky Lanky Liz see *Skinnigut*.

Swell-hide see *Jumbo*.

Swensker: is a general nickname given to a Swede in the Merchant Navy. It is simply a corrupt pronunciation of *Svenske*.

Swift: naval nickname for a member of the crew who is always last to turn out, and who is slow in his work and play. It is often rendered *Swifty*.

Swillocks: is a nickname given

to a person of intemperate habits. Lancashire dialect.

Swiss: is the American, shortened, form of Swiss Admiral. (See next entry.) A. A. Roback who records it in his *Dictionary of International Slurs* (1946) suggests it is influenced by many door-porters being of Swiss origin. In U.S.A. this may be so: in Britain Swiss nationals are not in excess, and the large number of Germans who claim to be Swiss deceive no one but themselves.

Swiss Admiral: is a jocular Cockney term of reference to a Linkman (door-porter) at a big restaurant, hotel, or picture theatre. It alludes to the gorgeous livery generally worn by these often well-to-do (on tips) and frequently arrogant and insolent nobodies. In the XIX C. it was naval slang for the professional beggars who infest yachting harbours, and invariably pretend to have held naval commissions.

Swotpot see *Enos*.

T

Tabernacle Tim: is the nickname used in the Navy for a man who is a self-appointed moralist and a lay-preacher; often a total abstainer and a non-smoker, with a mission to convert his mess-mates. They, for-

tunately, being miserable sinners, can keep smiling in spite of 'Tabernacle's' intolerance and gloom.

Tackline: naval nickname for a tall, thin man. A tackline is six feet in length.

Tad: an American nickname for any male person: particularly a little boy—sometimes *Little Tad*, and by inversion *Old Tad* for an old man. Sometimes applied to a person who will not pay his debts.

Tadpole: is an American nickname for a boy or girl whose parents came from France—a young *frog* [q.v.]. It is also—in U.S.A.—applied to citizens from Mississippi.

Taffy: inevitable nickname of any Welshman. Navy originally, adopted by the Army and ultimately by civilians. It is applied particularly to any man (Welsh or not) who is named Davis or Davies.

Tamale: is an American nickname for a Mexican girl.

Tambo: is the nickname of the performer in a negro-minstrel troupe, whose instrument is the tambourine.

Tan: is an American nickname for a Mulatto.

Tank see *Jumbo*.

Tankie: a member of the Armoured Corps. The term was employed chiefly by Australians: also a naval nickname applied to a Petty Officer or a Leading Seaman who is put in charge of the fresh-water tanks.

Taper see *Skinnigut*.

Tar-heel: a general nickname used in U.S.A. for anyone from North Carolina.

Tar pot: is an American

nickname originally bestowed upon negro children, later extended to include adults, now obsolescent.

Tarzan: is a general nickname for any man who is hairy and unkempt: for anyone who is big, round-shouldered and long-armed: for anyone who is self-assertive and rough, particularly in his dealings with women. It was, too, one of the nicknames by which Brigadier Orde Charles Wingate, leader of the *Chindits*, was known. From the character *Tarzan*, created by Edgar Rice Burroughs (1875–1950). He, Tarzan, was a super-active, super-he-man, accidentally reared by anthropoid apes; however, in spite of this advantage, when it came to junglecraft, Tarzan could teach Wingate nothing.

Tassie (Tazzy): general nickname for any man from Tasmania. Australian origin and usage.

Tax: a nickname employed at Tonbridge School says Morris Marples (*Public School Slang* (1940)), for 'those with projecting or staring eyes'.

Tea-cake: is one of the numerous inseparable nicknames attached to Smith. It seems to have been used in all the Forces during the Second War, but not to have survived in civilian life. Origin unknown.

Teague: a now obsolete nickname for any Irishman: from

this Irish surname which appears in the once very popular song 'Lillibullero'. Often pronounced Tig.

Tech: is the nickname bestowed upon a student of a *tech*nical subject at London (? other) University.

Tecker see *Nabby*.

Ted: during the Second War it was a nickname equivalent to *Jerry*, but used specifically by troops on the Italian front: from *Tedesco*, a German (Italian language).

After the war, when a sartorial-minded imbecile bribed a tailor to make him a suit of clothes cut in the style favoured during the reign of King Edward VII, and the mass-production slop-shops saw a chance to save cloth and so 'popularized' the style, all loungers, layabouts, juvenile delinquents and other undesirable characters, hitherto called 'corner-boys', had their generic nickname changed to 'Teddy-boys' and then reduced to Ted(s).

Teddy: was the affectionate nickname bestowed upon King Edward VII by his subjects who still employ it in reference to him and his times. It was also the nickname of Admiral Lord Mountevans—'Evans of the Broke' and it is the inseparable nickname of any man named Beare, when pronounced *Bare*, (but when pronounced Beer, see

Ginger). From the nickname of Theodore Roosevelt (1828–1919) twenty-sixth President of the U.S.A., after whom the popular 'soft-toy', known as a 'Teddy bear' was named. In U.S.A. it is a nickname for an Irishman.

Telegraph Pole: is a nickname that Cockneys used to give to tall, thin people, but now that most Post Office Telecommunication wiring is underground, the term is falling into desuetude.

Tenderfoot: is a nickname used derisively by the 'cowpokes' and other home-brewed Westerners, for anyone from the Eastern States who tries to compete in knowledge, skill and daring with the local folk.

Ten-ton see *Jumbo*.

Terrier(s): general nickname applied to any member of the Territorial Army. They, like other volunteers, were made the victims of public abuse and sarcasm in time of peace, but 'when the blast of war blows in our ears . . .'

Thing-a-my-bob see *Waznam*.

Thingame see *Waznam*.

Thingstable: is a nickname often given to a man named Constable. The reason is obvious: allied to the 1914–18 wartime catch-phrase 'Fighting for my country—only it don't grow on trees!'

Thinima see *Skinnigut*.

5

Threeo: nickname for a Third Officer in the W.R.N.S.

Three Ringer see *Ringer*.

Three-striper see *Striper*.

Tibby: is an endearing nickname given to a lively young girl in Suffolk dialect. In other parts of the country it is applied to a pet lamb, and in London to the cat.

Tich: is the inevitable nickname of any small man, but sometimes, by the humour of inversion, attached to a big man: from Little Tich, the Big-Booted Comedian, who flourished early XX C. His boots, which from heel to toe were the same length as himself from heel to crown, were articulated, and fitted with spring devices that enabled him to perform the most amazing feats from dancing to inclining forward at about forty-five degrees.

Tickler: is a nickname given to ordinary seamen by able seamen and other exalted personages up to petty officers. It is not intended to be accepted as a compliment, on the other hand, being meaningless, it is not exactly insulting.

Tiddler: is a general Cockney schoolboy's slang for the stickle-back (*G. Gasterosteus*) but before the 1914–18 war it was employed as a nickname for any boy who, although undersized, was particularly agile.

Tiddley: is the inevitable nick-

name of the eldest of three brothers at King Edward's School, Birmingham.

Tie mate: is now obsolete, but in the days when sailors wore pig-tails, two close friends were described as tie-mates.

Tig see *Teague*.

Tiger see *Midge*.

Timber: the most frequently employed nickname of men named Wood(s). It is commonly used in civil life as well as the Services, and is even known to have invaded girls' schools when there is a Miss Wood(s) among the mistresses.

Tin-ribs see *Skinnigut*.

Tiny: a nickname applied to abnormally big and powerful men: Rugby players and others. It is seldom applied to small men (cf. *Lofty*). It is an outstanding example of the process of humour by inversion.

Tiny Tim see *Midge*.

Titchie: is a nickname given to a master who enjoys using the *titch*, as the birch is named, at Christ's Hospital.

Titeems: is a nickname used in U.S.A. for an Englishman. From a French nickname meaning *tea time*.

Titman: is an American nickname for an undersized boy. It is sometimes bestowed by schoolmasters on the smallest boy in the class. It is Standard American English for the smallest pig in the litter: equivalent to Standard

British English *Runt* which is in U.S.A. regarded as dialect.

Tod: is the inseparable nickname of any man named Hunter. Tod is a Northern word meaning a fox: the origin, which is not Norse, remains unknown, but it occurs in literature as early as 1170 (O.E.D.). The word is now in verbal usage either dialect or slang; its status is, however, preserved in Heraldry where it serves in canting arms. *Toddy* in Northern dialect means heavy, from a wool-trade standard of weight; *toddy* in slang means 'foxy', cunning, hence either or both may have been formative. It is also applied to any man named Sloan, from the name of the famous jockey.

Tojo: a term of reference, and of address, to any Japanese soldier. Applied as a matter of course to prisoners: from Tojo, the politician who pushed Japan into the war.

Tolly: is a nickname, now obsolete, for the keeper of a toll-gate. There is no evidence that the keeper of the toll-gate still in operation at Dulwich, London, S.E. is so nicknamed by local people.

Tom: is the inseparable nickname of any man named King: from the XVIII C. highwayman. In mid-XIX C. it was a Cockney term of reference to a prostitute in which usage it survived up to 1914, but during the latter part of its life it was somewhat confused with, and overshadowed by, the 'better class' use as a nickname for a Lesbian.

Tom Thumb see *Midge*.

Tommy: is the XX C. nickname for all private soldiers. It became popular and public through the work of Rudyard Kipling, 'It's Tommy this, and Tommy that, and Tommy you're a hero,' but had been in use as a friendly term of address by soldiers, one to another, from *c.* 1830. The name originates in the first Army Pay Book, issued August 1815, called 'Soldier's Account Book' which had to be signed by the holder. At that time it was necessary to supply with it a 'specimen page', the written parts in script: the hypothetical name chosen was 'Thomas Atkins X his mark'. Later the 'X his mark' was omitted. The specimen page is no longer issued. The nickname is also a Cockney term of address to any little boy (under, say, twelve years old) whose name is unknown. 'Do your bootlace up, Tommy—you'll fall over.' It is the inseparable nickname of any man named Thomas or Thompson.

Tommy Tanner (or **Tanner**): 'nickname for a Kanaka working on a Queensland plantation; *c.* 1880–1920 (B[aker]., 1943)'. See E. Partridge, *A Dictionary of Slang—Supplement*.

Tony: general nickname employed during the 1914–18 war for any Portuguese. There was a Portuguese Expeditionary Force. During the Second War the nickname was transferred to Italian prisoners: from the given name, Antonio.

Toothpicks: nickname of the inhabitants of Arkansas, U.S.A.

Toothy: naval nickname for the ship's dentist.

Topper: is the inseparable nickname of any man named Brown. The origin is probably anecdotal: there is also a suggestion that it is from underworld slang; topper, the hangman; to be topped, to be executed; to be executed, to be 'done'; to be thoroughly, or well done, is to be 'done brown' (from cook's terms).

Topsy: inseparable nickname of any man named Turner: from *topsy-turvey*: chiefly naval. Also the inevitable nickname of the second in seniority of three brothers at King Edward's School, Birmingham. It is also a name likely to be given to any little girl whose own name is not known.

Torpoint Chick(en): the same as *Stamshaw Nannygoat* [q.v.].

Torps: naval nickname for the Torpedo Lieutenant.

Tory Rory: a London nickname given, *c.* 1780–1845, to 'those who wore their hats fiercely cocked'. (Eric Partridge, quoting J. Redding Ware.)

Tosh: the inseparable nickname of any man named either Gilbert or Harding, but more importantly a friendly and familiar term of address used by Cockneys to any male person of any age, and of any social status. Its attachment to Messrs. Gilbert and Harding is naval in origin and use, and may have reference to some once notorious partnership whose speciality was that of artists at 'the toshing lay': that is, the stealing of yellow-metal from ships' bottoms when so sheathed. It was a Cockney adventure, being most prevalent on London's River. In mid-XIX C. in Public School slang, a 'tosh-can' was a bath—probably of copper. This latter might be regarded as rhyming slang on *wash*. The word 'tosh' may be a shape of *tush*, which is dialect for *tuss*, a tusk, hence a tooth. When the nickname assumes the form *tusher* (as it frequently does) it supports the idea that it may have reference to the teeth hence, to eating (heartily) hence, to well-being hence, a complimentary nickname. Further, 'toshing' is *biting* the copper off the ships' bottoms. At Sandhurst 'tosh' is the nickname of a man with one leg. Perhaps from 'peg', a tooth.

Toshy: is a term of reference to, and a nickname for, a hairy-faced man. Yorkshire dialect. When a woman is referred to

as toshy it means that she is overdressed.

Tot see *Midge*.

Tottie: is the inseparable nickname of any man named Bell.
In dialect, that which is 'tottie'
is shaky: a bell must be shaken
to ring—there might be a connection. In South Africa it is
the nickname given to a Hottentot servant.

Tower of London: used by
children as a nickname for a
lanky boy. Recorded by I. and
P. Opie in *Lore and Language
of Schoolchildren* (1959). The
'tower' element suggests height;
it is not primarily a reference
to the Norman antique east of
the City of London.

Trader: is the inseparable nickname of men named Horn(e).
It is suggestive that from about
1680 to 1820, *a trader*, or *she-
trader* or a *trading-dame* was slang
for a prostitute.

Traik: is a term of reference
to, and a nickname for a slattern.
Scottish dialect.

Trapper see *Flatty*.

Trick cyclist: nickname originated in the Army for a
psychiatrist: now widely adopted.

Tricksy: is a nickname given
to a lively, tomboy-ish girl.

Trollybags: is a term of
reference to, and a nickname for,
a fat, dirty, uncouth person.
North of England dialect. As a
dialect word it refers to the entrails of sheep.

Trolly-mog: is a term of
reference to, and a nickname for,
a fat slovenly woman.

Trooker: is a term of reference to, and a nickname for,
a woman suspected of practising
witchcraft. Scottish dialect.

Trotter: is a nickname bestowed by Cockneys upon a
stranger settled among them who
has given no very satisfactory
account of his origin: from
trot, to proceed at a pace between
walking and running, hence the
inference is that the stranger
is 'on the trot', is a fugitive from
his native locality; one in hiding
from, say, a nagging wife or
the police, or insistent creditors;
one who is known to be (or
who untruthfully boasts of being)
a deserter from either the Navy
or the Army.

In the tailoring trade it is the
nickname of the runner—the
messenger who carries the sec-
tions of garments to and from the
out-workers. In Dublin it is the
nickname of a student, working
for a degree, without residence:
in Durham, of a day-student at
the University.

The Dickensian use, 'Trotty'
for Toby Veck the Ticket Porter
(*Chimes*) who invariably advanced at a trot, is still employed
in Covent Garden where it
is the nickname of an expert
barrow trundler.

Trugs: is a nickname given
to a lazy man. Scottish dialect.

Trunky: as a nickname for anyone with a prominent nose is less popular than *Conkey* [q.v.]. The term is comparative: an elephant's trunk being indicated.

Tubbelina see *Jumbo*.

Tubby: is an inseparable nickname for any man named Martin. It is also a general nickname for a broad-shouldered, deepchested short man. It is not applied to a fat man, nor to a pendulousbellied man. It is used in the Armed Forces, but is not specifically a soldier's (or a sailor's) term. It was bestowed upon the Rev. P. B. Clayton (now C.H., M.C., D.D.), the founder of Toc H. (Talbot House) during the First War, and by it he is known throughout the world. 'Tubby' is baby-talk for *Chubby*, and among the boys of Christ's Hospital it is a general nickname for a lavatory attendant.

Tubs see *Jumbo*.

Tubus see *Jumbo*.

Tuckoes: nickname applied to one from North Carolina, U.S.A.

Tug: is the inseparable nickname of any man named Wilson. It arises from the phonetical distortion of the nickname 'Chug', which was that of Admiral of the Fleet Sir Arthur Knyvet Wilson, V.C.

Tupper: is an alternative or an erroneous spelling of Topper [q.v.].

Turf-cutter: is an American term of reference to a person of Irish descent: from *turf*, peat.

Turk: is a general nickname in U.S.A. for an Irishman. Said to be from the Gaelic *torc*, a wild boar. It is transferred from the Irish to any quick-tempered person, and is often used as a specific nickname for a heavyweight boxer.

Turner: is an American general nickname for a German: from the name of a 'gymnasium' called *The Turners*.

Tut: is the inseparable nickname of any man named Pharaoh: it is a shortened form of *Tutankahmen*, the excavation of whose tomb aroused great popular interest.

Twenty - three - fifty - nine (hours): was a nickname used by British troops in the Far East for a coloured officer. 23.59 is one minute to midnight—as dark as can be.

Twinkle-toes see *Midge*.

Two-and-a-half Ringer see *Ringer*.

Two-and-a-half-striper see *Striper*.

Two-o: nickname for a Second Officer in the W.R.N.S.

Two Ringers see *Ringer*.

Two-striper see *Striper*.

Two-Ton-Tessie see *Jumbo*.

U

U-boat: is the nickname given to a round-shouldered rating. It originated during the 1914–18 war from the dome-like top of the conning-tower of the German submarine of the period. These vessels were distinguished by the letter 'U' and a number— i.e. 'U666'—not by name. ('U' for *Unterseeboot*, under-sea-boat.)

Uessayster see *Usian*.

Unc: is a Merchant Navy (passenger ships) nickname given by deck-hands to stewards. From their avuncular attitude to their patrons.

Uncle: a term of reference applied to a Pawnbroker: it may also be used in address if the pawnbroker (or assistant) is good-natured and friendly. It may be derived from *uncus*, a hook, on the assumption that goods pawned in Rome were lifted to the overhead store-room on a hook. The shaft through which goods make the ascent in modern times is called the 'spout' hence, goods pawned are said to be 'up the spout'. It is also a friendly nickname for an elderly man—even a stranger: in this latter usage it is not quite so popular as *Dad* [q.v.].

Uncle Sam: nickname for the entire American nation, and for a 'typical' American citizen. It is the nickname generally accepted on both sides of the Atlantic. Said to be derived from the initials U.S.

Underling: a nickname given to the under-butler at Felstead School. From the pun on Ling, the Butler.

Usanian see *Usian*.

Ushant: a nickname used in the Merchant Navy for a man with one eye: from the Ushant lights, one fixed, one flashing.

Usian: is an American nickname for any American citizen. From *U.S.-ian*. It takes several other forms on the same plan: *Usanian, Usonian, Uessayster*.

Usonian see *Usian*.

V

Vacher: an old (now obsolete) nickname for an American cowboy: from the French.

Velvet: is a nickname used chiefly in the underworld, for a man who specializes in ingratiating conversation with strangers: a 'contacts man'.

Vittles: the old Navy's nickname for the Victualling Paymaster.

W

Waak: or Wacc, from W.A.A.C. (*W*omen's *A*rmy *A*uxiliary *C*orps), being a general nickname for any member of that Service. During the 1914–18 war the recruiting poster, designed to shame slackers into joining, showing a child asking, 'What did *you* do in the Great War, Daddie?' was cryptically answered by the troops, 'I did my whack!' In spite of this, and thousands of other bawdy jokes, the moral standard was no lower than that set by civilian norms.

Wacky: is a term of reference to, and a nickname for, a fool. It is old Yorkshire dialect, but spelt *whacky*, and extended to cover circumstances as well as people, it is believed to be modern American. 'Whacky, like everything in the Big City, you can get tomorrow's paper today in New York.'

Wad: an old Navy nickname, current up to *c.* 1914 for either the Commissioned, or the Warrant Gunnery Officer. It originates in the wads used in breech-loading, powder and ball guns; later, the stoppers for guns were so named.

Wagstaff: is a child's nickname for a lanky boy. Recorded by I. and P. Opie in *Lore and Language of Schoolchildren* (1959).

Wahzit see *Waznam*.

Waler: is one of the nicknames given in both the Royal and the Merchant Navies to a Welshman. The word seems to be of early XIX Cent. American coinage.

Walking - lamp - post see *Skinnigut*.

Wank: is a nickname given, in the North of England, to a simpleton. It is seldom heard in the South of England, where the word has an altogether different connotation: however, *wonk* is a schoolboy's term of reference to a fool. (An object that is wonky is insecure.)

Water-rat: a waterfront underworld nickname for a member of the highly efficient Thames River Police.

Waterworks: is a shrewd Cockney nickname for a woman or child who, having conscious control of the lachrymal glands, uses the mechanism of floods of tears in both defence and attack. An example from English literature is that of 'the veepin' cove' of Margate Hoy—*Ingoldsby Legends*.

Wave(s): nickname for members of the W.A.V.E.S.: *W*omen's *A*uxiliary *V*olunteer *E*xpeditionary *S*ervice: the American equivalent of the British W.R.N.S.

Waxy: nickname for a saddler,

used in the old Cavalry and Horse Artillery. It is now obsolete.

Waznam (What is your name?) also, **Wahzit** (What is it?): These are primarily schoolboys' words used in addressing a newcomer whose name is as yet unknown; but either may become a permanent nickname if, when the revelation is made, the name proves difficult to assimilate or to pronounce. In London, names of foreign origin; Northern names, particularly those with the 'thwaite' suffix; and West Country names are likely to be replaced. Children have, with names, a kind of taboo system which is revealed by Iona and Peter Opie in *Lore and Language of Schoolchildren* (1959): 'Children attach an almost primitive significance to people's names, always wanting to find out a stranger's name, yet being correspondingly reluctant to reveal their own. They have ways of avoiding telling their names. They answer, "Haven't got a name, only got a number." They say, "Same name as me Dad." "What's your dad's then?" "Same as mine."[1]

Girls as well as boys have the same inhibition: '. . . there is a recurrent set-piece: "What's your name?" "Sarah Jane." "Where do you live?" "Down the lane."

[1] This footnote gives a French rhyme, printed 1883, using the same technique.

"What's your number?" "Cucumber." "What's your shop?" "Lollipop." "What's your town?" "Dressing-gown." This nameshyness extends to the U.S.A. A child's chant from Maryland, about a hundred years ago, was:

What's your name?
Pudd'n Tame.
Ask again
I'll tell you the same!'

Thing-a-my-bob (with several variants) is recorded in this usage by Dr. Harold Wentworth in *American Dictionary of Dialect*. It is also used in London and reduced to *Thingame*. *Dingus* appears to be solely American. Dr. Wentworth calls attention to *Word-list from Virginia*, the author's actual surname being Dingus (L.R.). Henry W. Shoemaker includes *Whatecallum* among his thirteen hundred oldtime words used in Pennsylvania, and surviving until 1930.

Weasels: nickname applied to persons from South Carolina, U.S.A.

Webfoot: is a nickname used in U.S.A. for a native of Oregon. From the high average annual rainfall in that State.

Weed see *Midge*.

Weevil Bo'son: naval nickname for the Victually Officer: it comes through from the days of mouldy biscuits and rancid pork.

Wee-wee: a now obsolescent

nickname for any Frenchman: from '*oui oui*'.

Welsher: an American nickname for a person of Welsh origin. It is a changed form of *Waler* [q.v.].

Welwyn: R.A.F. pilots' nickname for each other. (It does not refer to the Garden City Suburb of London, the name of which it puns.) Eric Partridge, in *A Dictionary of Forces Slang* 1939–45, says: '. . . its meaning and its origin are somewhat esoteric: c.f. *Pull your finger out*,' at which entry he says: 'Hurry up! Make a start! (Don't stand gaping with your finger in your mouth—well, that is the polite explanation.)'

Westo(e): naval nickname for a West Countryman.

Wetback: is an American term for a Mexican: assumed to be derived from the fact that illegal immigrants from Mexico swim across the Rio Grande.

Whacker: a term of address employed by gunners of the Royal Field Artillery, to each other. Equivalent to Mate, or Chum, or Tosh [q.v.]. Evolved during the Second War and perhaps having reference to *whack*, punish, smack, which is what the gunners were doing to the enemy. It is also an inseparable nickname for men named Pain or Payne. Naval. Punning on 'whack of'—share or portion or allowance of.

Whacky see *Wacky*.

Whatecallum see *Waznam*.

Wheeler: is the inseparable nickname of any man named Johnson.

Whelps: nickname of the inhabitants of Tennessee, U.S.A.

Whiskers: is a nickname given in the Navy, to any man who shaves blue: but, strangely enough, not to one having obtained permission 'to grow the full set'. It is also a term of reference to, and a nickname for, a little boy: further, it is an affectionate term of address to a cat and when thus used there is a tendency for it to be altered to *Whiskey*.

Whistler: is the nickname used during the Second War for female railway workers.

White hat: is a nickname used on the Thames waterfront for anyone named Willis: from *Old White Hat*, the nickname of Mr. John Willis, owner of clipper-ships (including *The Cutty Sark*) who always wore a white topper.

Whitey: is the inevitable nickname of a man whose hair is so fair that it is semi-albino.

Wholemeal: is a lesbian's term of reference to a girl or woman who is sexually normal. The inference is that wholemeal bread is baked from 'natural' flour.

Wiggy: is the inseparable nickname of any man named Bennett. This, in common with most, if not all, inseparables originated in the Navy, and is probably anecdotal.

Wilfred: is a nickname sometimes given to a teetotaller. From the name of Sir Wilfred Lawson (1829–1906) the British 'Pussyfoot'.

Wilkie: is one of the inseparable nicknames attached to the surname Collins. From Wilkie Collins, the novelist, famous for *The Woman in White*, etc. (1824–1889).

William Winter: was a nickname, now obsolete, given by all persons connected with 'show-business', to any drama critic. From the name of the *New York Tribune* critic (1836–1917).

Windmill: a nickname prefixed to the surname of a J.P. or other 'public figure' in Australia. In use to the end of XIX Cent., now obsolete. The inference was that the person so styled could neither read nor write, and used an X for a signature.

Wingco: is the nickname given to a Wing Commander, R.A.F.

Wingy: a nickname often given to a man with one arm. '*A wing*' was nautical slang for an arm ('flipper' for a hand) early in the XIX C. It was in use as a nickname as early as 1881, when it was recorded by Barrett.

Winky: is a nickname of an endearing character, given to a neat, dainty girl. From Scottish dialect *Winkey* (or *ie*) small, tiny.

Winlaton-shag see *Shag*.

Winnie: the affectionate nickname used by English-speaking men throughout the world for the Rt. Hon. Sir Winston Spencer Churchill, K.G. It originated in the Army during the war, and it is safe enough to prophesy that in future it will be the inseparable nickname of all men named *Churchill*—if not of all men named *Spencer*.

Woff: is the nickname given to members of the Women's Auxiliary Australian Air Force.

Wog: originally a Cockney boy's nickname for a boy with a mop of unruly hair, from *golliwog*, a grotesque doll; it became, during the Second War, a general nickname for a native of Egypt, and was spread to cover those of adjacent lands or of related ethnic groups. No reliance should be placed upon the etymology by which it is derived from: *w*ily *o*riental *g*entlemen.

Wolverine: a general nickname used in U.S.A. for anyone from Michigan.

Wom: is a nickname for a *W*ireless *O*perator *M*echanic, R.A.F.

Wonk see *Wank*.

Wooden nutmegs: nickname applied to the inhabitants of Connecticut, U.S.A.

Woodscud: is a term of

reference to, and a nickname for, a strong, energetic, romping boy or girl. Dialect usage.

Wop: is the nickname given to the *Wireless Operator* in the R.A.F. Not connected with *Wop*, an Italian, which is of American origin, and has a far wider currency there than in England. It is from the Neapolitan dialect *guappo*, a form of greeting.

Wopag: is a nickname for a *Wireless Operator Air-Gunner*, R.A.F.

Wormy (or **Worms**): a naval nickname for old salts set ashore and employed as gardeners in naval establishments.

Wrack: is the term of reference applied to any member of the *Women's Royal Army Corps*.

Wring: is a term of reference to, and a nickname for, a weak, puny child. Scottish dialect: it refers to the smallest pig in the litter.

Wurst: one of the nicknames used in U.S.A. for a German.

X

Xantippe: 'a Scold; the name of Socrates's scolding wife; who never could move his Patience tho' by premeditated and repeated Injuries. Whence it is used for any Shrew, or scolding, brawling Woman.' *The Universal Etymological Dictionary*—3rd edn., Nathaniel Bailey, 1737.

Y

Yabock: is a nickname given to a 'gabbing, talkative child' (Wright) Scotland.

Yank: a term of reference to any American citizen either in or out of the American Forces. It is a short form of Yankee, which was originally a term of contempt used by the Confederates for the Federals. It is now universal, and is neither used nor accepted as an insult.

Yap: is an American nickname for a Japanese. From a distortion of *Jap*.

Yarmouth bloater see *Bloater*.

Yellowbellies: a nickname applied to men of Wexford, Ireland, particularly by men of Wicklow; and a term of reference to, sometimes a nickname for, natives of Lincolnshire, England. The English usage is from the yellow ventral surface of eels (and frogs) in the fens.

Yelper: 'a Town-Cryer; also, one subject to complain, or make pitiful Lamentation for Trifling Incidents.' *The Universal*

Etymological Dictionary—3rd edn., Nathaniel Bailey, 1737.

Yodeller or **Yodelander**: is an American nickname for a person from Switzerland.

Yolky see *Eggy*.

Yorkshire tyke: is a term of reference applied to a Yorkshireman. It may be used as a term of address, but in only an unfriendly or a derisive setting.

Yorky: is a general nickname bestowed by Cockneys upon anyone from either Yorkshire or Lancashire. The Cockney ear does not detect the difference between the accents of the two counties, and the Cockney mind has no patience with topographical refinements: he who is not a Londoner is a countryman though he may come from one of the great provincial conurbations, and have as little knowledge of the country as a Cockney has.

The term comes out of the Army, and was current during XIX Cent. in London and in Home Counties regiments.

Young Shaver: is a term of address generally used patronizingly by older to younger men. From 'shaver', one who shaves. The term has been in general use since *c.* 1830, but can be traced as far back as 1630. *Old Shaver*, a man of experience, is used only by seamen.

Youngy: is an inseparable nickname for a man named Moor(e), or Muir. From *Old Moore's Monthly Messenger* (known as 'Old Moore's Almanac' or simply as 'Old Moore's'). 'Young' is by inversion of 'old'.

Younker: is a nickname sometimes given to a young man. It appears to be of more frequent use in U.S.A. than in England: as is *Oldster* for an elderly man.

Z

Zad: 'crooked, like the letter Z; as, *A meer Zad*, used of any bandy-legg'd, crouch-back'd, or deformed Person.' *The Universal Etymological Dictionary*—3rd edn., Nathaniel Bailey, 1737.

Zambuk: is a nickname commonly bestowed upon a person with a spotty face. It is from the name of a famous skin-ointment.

I. and P. Opie, in *The Lore and Language of Schoolchildren*

(1959), give 'Bumps, Dimples, Crater-face, Freckles, Frecklefaced-faggot, Leopard, Mealyface (hence "School Dinners"), Measle nob . . . Pepper pot, Pimple bonce, Poxie and Scabbyguts' (p. 171).

Zaygeh: is a Cockney-Yiddish nickname for anyone. It is often used by Jews to call attention to (say) a child performing some interesting feat, who will (or may) desist if he realizes he is noticed: the phrase is 'Cook at [look at] Zaygeh!' The same phrase would be employed by a Jewish stall-holder to call the attention of his neighbour (Jew or Gentile) to a person examining the goods and judged to harbour thievish intentions. It is a term of reference to, and a nickname for, anyone of minor intelligence, acting in a humble capacity, in the Cockney-Jewish world: for example, a tailor's workshop 'runner', or the scavenger who sweeps the market. It is applied to both Jews and Gentiles. From *Zaygeh*, Yiddish for a clock hence, a face, and extended to the whole person.

Zaufer: is a Yiddish-Cockney nickname for a greedy person.

Zelda: is a nickname given by beatniks and similar undesirables to any middle-aged respectable woman, but particularly to a spinster.

Zero: is a nickname bestowed upon an inferior, humble person who makes a living by doing odd jobs (generally rather badly), and is a burden on the community. The term, which is American in origin, is there used frequently; in England but seldom.

Zigaboo: is an alternative spelling of *Jigaboo* [q.v.].

Zombie: is a Canadian nickname for men of the Home Guard. From the Voodoo belief that dead men can be bewitched into mechanical activity. In U.S.A. applied to a policeman.

Zucke see *Sukie*.

REVERSE REFERENCE

THE following list includes the names, states, mental and physical characteristics, places of nativity, and other peculiarities that attract the nicknames, terms of address, and terms of reference recorded in the foregoing Glossary. Names are printed in italic: a precaution made necessary by there being so many names that are not names alone—even *Smith* is the description of the craftsman who works iron or other metals.

It will be observed that some entries in the glossary are represented in this list twice, each time under a different heading: for example, 'blond hair', 'hair, blond'. This repetition is deliberate; the aim is to accommodate readers who approach their problem from different points of view. The author trusts he has anticipated his readers' requirements, but in the event of the information sought not appearing, the patient searcher is advised to try from a different angle.

If an item does not appear at all in this list, but is, notwithstanding, actually covered in the glossary, it is an error for which the author offers his apologies; if, however, it is a nickname not included in the work, it is an omission due to the ignorance of the author, who will be most grateful to those who enlighten him.

abdominal fat, 24, 41, 43, 46
able seaman, 106, 110
absent-minded person, 57
Accounting Officer (naval), 80
acne, one suffering with, 14, 104, 121
active person, 80, 99, 110, 113
actress, 61
Adams, 35, 91
Adjutant, 33
Admiral, the, 89
advice, giver of, 59, 60
agitator, 12, 23, 89, 106
aggressive person, 45, 49, 73, 97, 103, 108
Airfield Control Officer, 79
Alabama, natives or inhabitants of, 43, 63
Alban, 5
Alice, 61
Allonby, Cumberland, natives or inhabitants of, 97
ambitious Cadet, 2
America, Southern Continent, natives of, 14
American Citizen, 8, 13, 14, 27, 55, 56, 115, 120
American Indian, 8, 71
　male child, 58
　Marine, 53
　private soldier, 31, 39, 92
　sailor, 42
　Waves, 116
anti-gas instructor, 83
anti-modern, 90
anyone, 11, 12, 15, 17, 18, 21, 22, 23, 26,
41, 48, 49, 50, 52, 54, 55, 66, 75, 81, 84, 87, 96, 104, 105, 108, 112, 117, 121
appetite, robust, 32, 40, 46, 50, 76
Arkansas, natives or inhabitants of, 3, 43, 57, 88, 112
Armament Supplies Officer, 3
Armoured Corps, member of, 108
Armstrong, 95
arrogant person, 23
Artificer engineer, 105
Asdic Officer, 84
Assistant Director Ordinance Services, 2
Assistant Group Officer, 2
auburn hair, 6, 14, 18, 24, 42, 57, 66, 89, 90, 91
Australian aborigine, 53
　citizen, 8, 29, 78, 102
　immigrant, 53, 55, 86
　public figure, 119
　soldier, 2, 3, 29
　militiaman, 106
　squatter, 53
Auxiliary Territorial Service, member of, 3
Avery, 4
Azores, native of, 89

bad-tempered person, 10, 36, 70, 73, 74, 103, 104, 106, 114
Baker, 31, 38, 48, 102, 103
baldness, 4, 27, 32, 33, 79, 97
Ball, 43
Baltimore, natives or inhabitants of, 4

handsome woman, 61
Harding, 112
Harris, 11, 19
Hastings fishermen, 20
hat, small size in, 84
head, large, 8, 12, 33
Henderson, 44
henpecked, one who is, 7, 70
Henriques, Sir Basil, 40
Herring, 36
Hewett, 75
Highland soldier, 59
Hill, 54
Hinds, 25
Hingham (Mass.), natives or inhabitants of, 14
hire-purchase account collector, 31, 56, 57
Holland, 32
hollow cheeks, 48
Holloway, 83
Holmes, 100
homosexualist, 78
honest man, 81
Hook, 67
Horn(e), 86, 113
hotel guest, 55
Hottentot, 113
Hudson, 44, 102
Hughes, 37, 103
humorist, 27, 34, 78, 83
hunchback, 90
Hungarian person, 11, 44, 50
Hunter, 111
Hutch, 88
Hutchins. 88
Hutchinson, 88
Hynds, 25
hypocrite, officer who is a, 18, 34, 52

Idaho, natives or inhabitants of, 27, 38
idler, 59
Illinois, natives or inhabitants of, 106
  Southern, natives or inhabitants of, 33
immigrant, 53, 55, 104
impudent person, 63, 101
Indian (American), 8, 71
  (Asiatic), 89
Indiana, natives or inhabitants of, 49
Indiana Sect, 89
indiscreet person, 9, 40
inferior mental powers, 11, 17, 31, 38, 48, 51, 56, 66, 68, 74, 75, 84, 116, 122
initials 'H.C.', 50
initials, numerous, one with, 2
inquisitive person, 37, 74, 76, 80, 101
insignificant person, 6, 8, 26
intolerant person, 39
intrepid officer, 48
intruder, 16
Iowa, natives or inhabitants of, 27, 48
Irish girl, 7, 23, 79

man, 5, 6, 19, 36, 45, 48, 51, 68, 72, 73, 79, 80, 95, 104, 108, 114
rebel, 26
irritable person, 18, 25, 70
Italian civilian, 29, 42, 45, 52, 78, 88, 98, 103
  soldier, 66, 112
Ivory, 4

Jackson, 105
Jackson, General Thomas Jonathan, 105
Japanese person, 54, 74, 97, 120
  soldier, 111
Jarvis, John, Earl St. Vincent, 53
jaunting-car driver, 53
Jew, 1, 3, 33, 43, 48, 51, 57, 59, 70, 71, 86, 95, 96
  (Spanish), 40
Jewish convert, 6
  girls, 7
Johnson, 118
Jones, 42, 57
Jordan, 32
Juke(s), 51
juvenile delinquent, 109

Kanaka, 111
Kane, 106
Kansas, natives or inhabitants of, 53
Kathleen, 25
Kell(e)y, 74, 103
Kent, 31
Kentucky, natives or inhabitants of, 23, 24, 59
Kettle, 17
Kidd, 17
Kilkenny, natives or inhabitants of, 18
King, 76, 111
Knight, 11, 67, 75
knock-kneed man, 5
Knott, 72
Korean, 91

lascivious person, 89, 106
Lamb, 16
lamb, pet, 110
lamp-trimmer, 61
Lancashire man, 48, 62, 121
landlady, 30, 65
large head measurement, 12
latecomers, 72
Latin race, one of, 103
lavatory attendant, 27, 29, 114
Lawson, Sir Wilfred, 119
lazy person, 17, 37, 57, 63, 91, 102, 107, 113
Leach, 105
Leading seaman, 49, 59, 108
Lee(s), 11, 42, 55
Leech, 105
left-handed person, 17, 22, 62, 97
Legg, 81
Leicestershire man, 6

INDEX